For the Love of
MANX KIPPERS
(& Queenie Scallops)

The Ups and Downs of Commercial Fishing in the Isle Of Man

Mike Smylie

Of all the fishes in the sea,
the Herring is the King.
And all the sellers of the grog,
Rejoice when he comes in.

– Old Manx Ballad

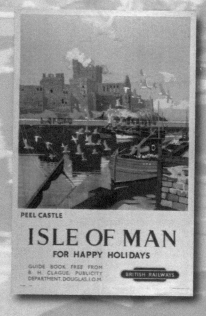

PEEL CASTLE

ISLE OF MAN
FOR HAPPY HOLIDAYS

GUIDE BOOK FREE FROM
B. H. CLAGUE. PUBLICITY
DEPARTMENT. DOUGLAS. I.O.M.

BRITISH RAILWAYS

Lily
Publications

Contents

Chicken Rock, the sentinel
to the south of the Island,
often the first sighting for
sailors from the south, and
now bringing back
memories of many a sail
across from Anglesey in
my younger days.

Introduction

I cannot start at the beginning, and have no wish to, for fishing most likely has been practised around the coasts of the Isle of Man since when prehistoric man first came here and I can't delve that far back. What I can do is allow readers a glimpse into windows over two hundred years or so, brief time capsules if you want, of the various fisheries, and ancillary offshoots, that involved many Manx folk. And many it did for in 1883, at the huge International Fisheries Exhibition in London, the Isle of Man was well represented by over 40 companies. According to the guide that was published along with volumes of academic papers, one in four of the Manx population were dependent, directly or indirectly, on fishing for their daily bread whilst at the same time one in five were dependent on it for their means of earning. In Britain as a whole, the average for the latter was one in every 75.

In a book of this type it is impossible to include the multitudinous amount of factors and variants that go to make up what can be termed 'the Manx fisheries'. I can only provide these brief windows that give both a personal representation and short history. I can only apologise, for detail sometimes has to be left to others and the wealth of local history of the fishery is immense. Foreigners to the Island such as me can only give an oversight, which I hope to have done, although I know there are many people who will have a far greater wealth of knowledge in particular areas of fishing. I have no pretence there for I have little links to the Island, the only ones being that my grandfather owned the Smylie's cash and carry in Douglas until the 1970s! However, I have visited often, especially in my younger years, and the Island holds a distinct string of memories that I continue to carry around. This book has given me the chance to relive some of them.

As usual various people have helped: Mike Craine, my co-founder of the 40+ Fishing Boat Association, is a mine of information which he gladly shares, as well as showing me around the Island. Thanks to artist Nicola Dixon who has helped brighten up Peel's central car park, Alex Ironside for welcoming me aboard his vessel, along with his crew Kelvin and Alex. Roy Baker of the Leece Museum for coming up with a book I'd been after. Paul Desmond for sharing kipper tales whilst the kiln smoked. Brian Cain for relating some of his memories. Wendy Thirkettle and wonderful staff at the Manx Museum for patience. Michael Teare for encouragement and opening up a company history. Fiona and John of Knockaloe Beg Farm for housing me. And finally my family for support whilst I was away.

For photos there's Alan Kelly of Mannin Collections, Pauline Oliver who gave me some 20 years ago, Darren Purves who has an excellent eye, and again Mike Craine and Nicola Dixon.

For Ana and Otis, as promised, for letting me escape to the hills once again to complete this book.....

The Early Herring Fishery

Herring – *y skeddan* in Manx – is the King of the Sea (*Ree ny marrey*). This fish, like no other, comes into various Manx household sayings of old: *Gyn skeddan, gyn bannish* (no herring, no wedding) or *Palchey phuddase as skeddan dy liooar* (plenty potatoes and herring enough). Herring was the national Manx diet, like it was throughout Scotland and Ireland, parts of Wales and England. So you would be quite normal thinking that 'at first there was herring, and only herring, and all fishermen went out in their little boats, fishing only to catch herring'.

But that's not correct. Read that and you'd be forgiven for thinking that fishermen never caught any other fish. They did, you know; it was not just herring! But when we read about the history of fish, this is often the perceived message that comes across. Of course our early fishermen landed other fish. However, what is true is that the herring fishing was the

Smacks drift-netting for herring.

7

A Manx *scowte* with single square sail in true Norse fashion.

first true 'fishery of consequence', as against just landing a multitudinous supply of whatever came into the net, or onto the hook.

The first great herring fishery is said to have taken place off the southern Swedish coast in the fourteenth century, only to pass to the Low Countries when the herring altered their migration route. Scotland then commanded it in the late eighteenth and nineteenth centuries, with Wick being known as the herring capital of Europe in the mid-1800s, as the North Sea continued to account for the majority of fish landed. Scottish boats chased the shoals southwards, culminating, once joined by English vessels, in the Great Autumnal herring fishery off East Anglia late in the year. But, for sure, there was more to it than those few sentences. Scotland's west coast was eagerly fished, as was the west side of Ireland. Shoals also flooded into the Irish Sea.

Which was great for the Isle of Man, centred nicely in that Sea. Not only that, but a superior herring migrated into the Irish Sea, similar to that of Loch Fyne which was considered of best quality. Herring spawn off the Manx coast, especially liking the coral seabed on the Douglas Banks on the southeast side of the island, although rich picking grounds were found on the opposite side and in the deeper water between the Island and the Irish coast, some thirty-odd nautical miles away to the WNW.

It is said that it was the Scottish who taught the Manx to fish, probably because of the Scots' rule of the Island in the thirteenth century. Thomas, Bishop of Sodor, was the first to mention 'the strangers in the herring fishery' in regard to taxes paid by these fishers, which assumes a fishery attracting outsiders. That was in the first half of fourteenth century. More documented evidence followed as the time ticked along.

What is perhaps more interesting from the point of view of today is the way the fishery was run. It was almost like a military operation, with the fishermen being controlled by Water Bailiffs and Admirals of the Herring Fleet. This tradition is said to have come from the days of the Norse kings. Indeed, the 1610 *Manx Statue Book* lists a long passage of regulations that ensured those fishing were under tight discipline. That fishermen were only seasonal is attested by 'the requirement for the more substantial, or 'quarter-land'

The smack *Maria* of Port St. Mary which was registered in 1789. This size of vessel would carry herrings to mainland England and further afield. Larger smacks sailed to the Mediterranean.

farmers to provide eight fathoms of nets fitted with corks and buoys in readiness for the fishing'. The start date of fishing was decided by regulation, and the masters of boats had to muster their vessels at the prescribed place at the requisite time. The vessels themselves, the herring *scowtes*, are described in a later chapter.

The Lancashire-born royalist landowner and topographer William Blundell (1620-1698), who lived on the Island in the 1650s, wrote of how fresh herring was the staple diet of the people who didn't know anything about red herrings – i.e. smoked herrings. 'The sea feedth more Manksmen than the soil', he stated[1]. But his evidence also supports the hard life of fishermen who were largely exploited. Once the herring was landed, 20% went to the Lord of the Isle, 20% to the church and some to the Water Bailiff whose job it was to supervise the fishermen at his court that he held once a week during the herring season. That meant that almost half the value of the catch had disappeared almost before it was landed. For the five or six crew, and the skipper and/or boat's owner, that didn't leave that much behind.

Double-ended yawls at Giant's Causeway. Similar vessels worked all over the Irish Sea and all stem from Norse influence.

The herring tower at Langness which is said to be a lookout tower for herring although it has also been described as a landmark for shipping. It was built in 1811.

It was the Admiral of the Herring Fleet who reported to the Water Bailiff any misdemeanours at sea such as shooting nets at the wrong time or cutting across someone else's nets, which would then be dealt with at the next court session. There was a Vice-Admiral as well, and both were appointed by the Water Bailiff. They were taken on for the duration of the fishing season and, in 1798, paid £5 and £2 respectively by the government.

The Admiral and Vice-Admiral had distinguishing flags on their boats. Nets could only be shot at night, and so the

Admiral lowered his flag to show when shooting could commence, and vice-versa at dawn. Woe betide those that flaunted the fishing regulations. And don't think about not turning out to fish. In July 1705 the skippers of some 14 boats from Kirk Bride were hauled before the court after being charged to go to the herring fishing at Port Erin and 'to have their nets and buoys and other things pertaining to the said fishing in good order'. The inference is that they failed to turn up at the beginning of the fishing and that their fishing gear wasn't up to scratch!

Blundell also notes that other fish were being caught but that herring was the prime source of their income in that they exported it to all four neighbouring countries as well as to France. The other fish he mentioned were salmon, cod, haddock, mackerel, rays, plaice, thornbacks, ling, crabs, lobsters and cockles. The cod, thornbacks and plaice, he wrote, were dried in the sun. More on this fishing in another chapter.

It's worth noting that, up to 1765 when the British Crown took control over the Island, goods were brought in after paying a very low import duty which allowed a flow of 'free trade' towards the other four adjacent countries – what from the Crown's point of view was considered as smuggling. It was a lucrative trade, and many fishermen with access to boats benefitted from the Island as being the central storehouse, as many regarded it. But during the fishing season, the herring always took preference.

Other regulations regarding the duties of fishermen are fascinating. When finding a shoal of herring, the crew of that boat were required to pass this information to their nearest boat and in this way this fact was transmitted to the whole fleet. Imagine that today when fishermen remain silent about their fortunes whilst fishing, or fabricate stories in complete reversal of these. Another law of 1737 states that herring cannot be exported until the Island people were fully supplied at a price not exceeding 1s. 2d. per hundred. In lean years herring was imported to satisfy local demand.

In the late eighteenth century it has been said that there were up to almost 400 boats sailing 'in and out of Douglas every day' which shows that the east coast fishery was centred in the port there. Every weekday most of them set out before sunset when the weather was fair, ready to cast their nets as the sun dipped below the western horizon in time with the Admiral's flag. It was on such a night that they sailed forth on 20th September 1787.

There's one such tower set amongst the apartments on Douglas Head (what was Douglas Head Hotel) though its use as a herring tower seems doubtful. Furthermore there's another behind the Villa Marina on the Central Promenade in Douglas (pictured here) as well as the tower in the grounds of Peel Castle, though the latter is believed to have been a tower of refuge...??

The St. Matthew's Day Douglas Bay Disaster

In 1787 the harbour at Douglas was very different to how it is today. It consisted of little more than a small section of pier somewhere outward from today's swing bridge, adjacent to the Isle of Man Steam Packet's present loading quay, at what was then the confluence of the river Glass. The southern edge of what was termed the harbour's lake was lined with rocks or a gravelly beach. At the end of the pier there was a brick lighthouse some 30-40ft high, 'lighted each night by seven or eight half-pound candles with a tin circular deflector behind them at about eight feet, and could be seen at the distance of four or five leagues at sea'[2].

The pier was described as a 'rude structure' by the then harbourmaster Mr. Nicholas Christian, and that it was composed of small stones which each easterly gale would displace and which needed constant repair. In 1786 a gale demolished some 84 yards of this pier, including the lighthouse. A temporary lantern on a pole on what remained of the pier was all the boats had to steer in by.

On the morning of the 20th September an unusually huge catch of herrings was landed and the weather was 'beautifully fine'. In the evening the herring fleet numbering up to 300 boats, maybe more, set sail for the herring grounds off Clay Head and Laxey.[3]

One eye witness was Mr. David Robertson who also noted the weather as being 'beautifully serene, the sky pure and unclouded'. but then 'at midnight a brisk equinoctial gale arose, and the fishermen, impelled by their usual temerity, fled to the harbour of Douglas'. Almost immediately the 'wretched substitute' of a light was destroyed by one of the first boats coming in, presumably by the heeled tip of the mast hitting it. Once extinguished, there was no way for any boat to find the safety of the harbour.

"The consequences were dreadful', said Mr Robertson. 'In a few minutes all was horror and confusion. The darkness of the night, the raging of the sea, the vessels dashing against the rocks, the cries of the fishermen perishing in the waves, and the shrieks of the women ashore, imparted such a sensation of horror, as none but a spectator can possibly conceive. When the morning came it presented an awful spectacle; the beach and rocks covered in wrecks, and a group of dead bodies floating in the harbour. In some boats whole families perished. The shore was crowded with women, some in all the frantic agony of grief, alternatively weeping over the corpses of father, brother, and husband; and others, sinking in the embrace of those, whom, a moment before, they imagined were buried in the waves.'

Mr Robertson and other writers do not specify how many boats were lost but it has been determined from fishery returns that between 50 and 60 boats were probably either totally destroyed or made unfit for repair. 21

fishermen are said to have died.

No wonder that these open boats were described as 'our poor shells'. However, the disaster did serve to persuade fishermen to build more seaworthy vessels and they eventually adopted the idea of decking them over, either partially or wholly.

But this was not the first disaster to hit fishing fleets around the UK coast, and not the last. But for the small Isle of Man it was extremely tragic, its hand stretching wide over the Island. Thus, for a century afterwards, none of the Manx fishing communities would fish on the anniversary of the Douglas Bay disaster.

It took until 1793 for the foundation stone of a new pier to be laid, and the work was not completed until 1801 which, the following year, was described as having a 'handsome lighthouse' on a short pier[3].

A Century of the Herring 1780-1880

The immediate effect of the wrecking of such a large number of boats, and the tragic loss of life that accompanied it, was twofold. Firstly the design of boats was put under the microscope, with the obvious being the lack of a deck to protect the crew, and secondly there was a sudden awareness of the inadequate harbour facilities. For perhaps the first time the fishermen saw their open boats for what they were: shells. Indeed this had been said many years before. A clash between four Whitehaven buss-type fishing boats and 100 Manx boats in 1753 ended with the Manx objecting to the strangers fishing their waters, and a reply from the Duke of Atholl's office to Whitehaven wrote that 'your busses will behave carefully, tenderly and cautiously towards our poor little shells...so as not to distress them.' In other words, over 30 years before the Douglas disaster there

A typical herring buss.

An Irish Sea wherry sailing into Maryport. These sort of vessels were commonplace around both the English and Irish coasts, as well as working the Manx waters. Print in William Daniell's *A Voyage around Great Britain*, 1815.

was a realisation by the authorities that the boats were unseaworthy.

Smacks had been trading with the Island for many years and the fishermen adopted this type of boat, though of course not over night. It was a slow change-over but had the added advantage of allowing them to sail further in their quest for fish. The fore-and-aft rig was handier, though some preferred the schooner-rigged wherries that the free-traders had adopted, and the same vessels were used by the 'fresh buyers' of the herring to carry it straight back to Liverpool and Dublin. It has been estimated that in 1800 there were 40 to 50 'fresh buyer' boats. Larger smacks delivered the herring as far away as the Mediterranean.

Press gangs were a constant threat to the ability of boats to find crew. The Navy had long seen fishermen as a good addition to its crewing needs, given their seaborne experience. Thus they scoured the fishing grounds, often taking away crews, leaving one to sail home. However the authorities attempted to restrain the navy ships from impressing the 'landowners employed in the Manx Herring

Fishery'.[4] Not sure how successful that was!

By the 1800s there was a considerable amount of herring being landed and the Red Herring houses of the Island kept busy. One report states that there were between 400 and 500 boats in the Manx fleet in 1811 but that these were still not decked over which tends to contradict what is said above. Presumably some were, some weren't. This trade in cured fish continued until the 1830s, a time which coincided with the loss of the West Indies slave market on the abolition of slavery in 1833.

Then, in the 1840s, things started to change as boats from outside the Irish Sea began to come and fish the waters around the Island. Some say the Manx fishermen were part-timers, sharing their working life as farmers, until about 1840.[5] When these strangers came in their larger, decked over, better equipped boats, boats that needed a higher investment which in turn meant longer fishing seasons, fishermen had to work their boats as much as possible. Longer fishing seasons, in turn, meant they too had to sail to far away places outside the traditional Manx fishing season. At the same time a recovery in the home herring fishery meant that there were those willing to risk the higher investment. Boat numbers increased as the fishermen

Postcard view of Manx luggers lying in Port Erin bay. Although called luggers, they were dandy rigged with a lug mizzen.

19

turned to their larger dandy-rigged boats, and then to the larger luggers, built on Cornish lines and christened 'nickeys'.

By the 1860s many boats were going to the Kinsale mackerel fishery off Southern Ireland, a lucrative fishery in the spring where ultimately they could earn more than for the home herring fishing. The first boats had gone in 1861 and later joined some 800 vessels from Cornwall, Ireland, Scotland and France. Others sailed north to fish herring off Stornoway or Lerwick in Shetland, all to return to the Island for the summer and autumn herring. There were reports of some smacks going to the Killibegs herring at Christmas time. Fishing had, for the first time, become a sort of nomadic lifestyle!

In 1864 the Manx fleet was getting close to 300 first-class vessels above 15 tons of varying sizes – 170 in Peel,

'Making Red Herrings'.

Entrance to Castletown
harbour with the
herring tower in the
background.

A view across the river at Peel. In the foreground is the nickey *Twin Sisters*, PL39.

120 in Castletown which included Derbyhaven, Port St. Mary and Port Erin, and a few odds and sods. Ramsey and Douglas had none.[6] The same report tells us that the cost of a herring boat – presumably a nickey – cost £150 with another £100 for the nets. By 1870 the nickeys had almost completely superseded the older dandy-rigged boats.

From this it is easy to see that the fishing nets were of considerable expense and thus always looked after. When used every day, any holes would always be repaired and once a week or so the cotton nets would be taken ashore and barked: i.e. put in a high tannin solution of 'cutch' (or catechu) which helped preserve against the rot of the sea water. A solution of boiled oak bark was previously used until the treacle-toffee-like cutch was imported from India and became widely available. These nets were 2000 yards long, and 300 to 400 meshes deep. Before 1854, nets were made of flax or hemp which were often made at home by the womenfolk. They were made into 'jeebins' which were 52 meshes deep and 17 yards long. Sixteen of these formed a net, i.e. four deep by four along. If a mesh shrank, then it would be discarded, and the jeebins made replacement relatively simple. If an English shilling passed freely through between knot and knot, then the mesh was considered sufficient.

In 1854 though, Robert Corrin changed all this when he brought over a net-making loom to Peel from Scotland and began the cotton net-making business on the Island which later spread to Port St. Mary. The cottage industry of net-making disappeared almost immediately. Because mackerel and herring needed different nets – herring nets floated below the surface whilst mackerel nets were on the surface, the latter being heavier and a greater mesh, two more Peel net-makers soon opened up for business.

Nickeys at Port St. Mary. Amongst then are: Shah, CT1 and *Sensation* ,CT14, *May Queen*, CT29, *Wesley*, CT71, *Faithful*, CT77, *Honey Bee*, CT85, and *Edwin*, CT113.

In the share system used to split the earnings, once the herrings were sold, the provisions of the vessel were subtracted and the rest divided into 20 shares. Ten went to the owners of the net, 7½ to the crew and 2½ to the boat itself for maintenance.

The period 1870 to 1880 was the peak of the herring trade when there were said to be 1000 boats working the 'Channel fishery', regarded by many Manx fishers as 'our' channel. 300 were Manx, 120 from Campbeltown, 140 from Arklow, 150 from the East of Scotland, 200 from Cornwall and 100 from other Irish ports.

Such was the volume of fish being caught that mainland England was being supplied with fresh herring whilst salted herring was still being taken to the Baltic. On the other hand red herrings had declined to almost nothing yet hardly any was being smoked as kippers. However that was about to change.

Peel's Boom and Bust Years

Peel, in 1883, was a bustling, up-and-coming little town. From being described as having 'few houses placed in such a straggling manner and only one part which can be called a street' in 1802[7], eighty years later it was the main fishing port of the Island, having a fleet of over 300 boats, active shipyards, sail-makers and net-making workshops. The boats they were fishing with were considered the best and of the 300, 194 were first-class boats, 35 second-class boats and the rest small open third-class boats. Steam winches had been fitted to 40 nickeys, thus making the job of hauling in easier and quicker with the added advantage of allowing longer nets to be shot in the first place. But mechanisation had its effect on people: one man less was generally needed as crew.

1883 was the year of the International Fisheries Exhibition in London where the Island was well represented. Peel, according to the official guide, had 1,727 men and boys employed in the fishing whereas the south (Castletown, Port St. Mary and Port Erin) only employed 787. Douglas employed 119 folk and Ramsey 219. It was

Peel harbour with much of the fishing fleet of nickeys moored up.

25

from these statistics where the total of those employed in fishing was 2,872 (they added 20 for lobster fishing), and with another 700 employed as boatbuilders, sail-makers, net-makers, rope-makers, coopers and fish curers, the guide reckoned that this represented some 13,000 people who were reliant on fishing for their livelihood out of a total population of 53,000.

A recent addition had been the railway from Peel to Douglas (1877), from where steamers took the fresh catch to various destinations. Speed was essential to ensure the herring stayed fresh. And the ironic thing was that at the beginning of that decade, the Manx herring had seen another decline in its fortunes.

A fantastic source of information on the Peel herring fishery comes from a series of articles in the Peel City Guardian in 1987/88, which author and historian Fred Palmer gleaned from old issues of that paper. It states that in 1882 some 120 vessels had been built in Peel shipyards over a five year period. There were 'three net factories employing several hundred men and women', as well as there being 'ropeworks, sail lofts, shipsmiths, [net-] barkers, etc., making

The nickey *Xema*, PL37, leaving Peel.

At the upper end of the harbour there was always a bustle of activity. Here the harbour is dried out.

the weekly wages paid far more in proportion to the inhabitants than any town in the Island'. House building was up with 16 houses under construction whilst others were in the offing. 'Better class visitors who are now preferring the salubrious climate of this side of the Island' were fuelling this demand, a sign that tourism was about to flourish, at, to some extent, the expense of the fishing.

The paper of the time was full of fishing reports. Thus, on 28th July 1883, we find that 'about 80 boats left for the fishing grounds on Monday evening. The night was fine, with a light breeze from the N.N.W. They were up in a good time on Tuesday morning having a good night's fishing. The average number of fish was about 8 mease per boat, and they ranged from 40 mease down. The price was good, 26/- per mease being realised. About 500 mease in all were sold this day.' The following day the price reduced to about £1 per mease and by the Wednesday this had ranged from 23/- to 32/-, illustrating the fluctuations the fishers had to deal with. By Thursday only 50 boats went out and the fishing

The breakwater with steam drifters unloading herring, with barrels stacked high.

was poor with the average catch being 2 mease. Presumably the rest of the fleet was working the summer herring further north from Scottish ports.

A nickey, along with sails and herring and mackerel nets, cost in the region of £700 about this time which was a heavy investment, especially at a time when catches were declining. The cause of this decline was eagerly debated. Herring have been known to change their migration at a moment's notice, only to return a few years later. Yet some blamed over fishing whilst others said it was God's wrath over Sunday fishing and shooting nets before sunset. Many thought it was due to bottom trawling over spawning grounds and all might have contributed to poorer yields. Nevertheless new boats continued to be built, sometimes with the help of finance from Teare and Sons.

Teare and Sons were ships' chandlers and sail-makers. The business had been set up in about 1866 by Peel-born rope maker John Teare and his son William, a sail-maker, both of whom worked in premises on the Quay at Peel. Corks were cut for nets whilst the sail loft was also the store for the corks as well as rope, chain, paint, linseed oil, paraffin and petrol, as well as other items any skipper had ordered from away. In 1880 the company had 120 fishing boats on their books and these were able to buy goods on credit for six to twelve months. The company flourished and the profits were ploughed back in to purchase shares in fishing boats, as well as advancing wages when families were in need during periods of poor fishing. They also invested in property, owning one pub, the Oddfellow Arms (now the Creek Inn) and several dwelling houses which, excepting the ones they lived in, presumably were rented out. It wasn't just booze the fishermen had on credit!

As I write this, I conjure images in my mind of what the premises must have looked like and I can almost smell the Stockholm tar from the rope, the linseed oil and the fumes from the petrol, as well as hear the rustle of the heavy cotton sails and the chatter of the voices as fishermen relate their tales of the fishing. I can imagine that the sail loft was a magnet to the elder fishermen, those relegated to working small open boats for long-lining and potting.

In the 1880s the days of the big luggers were over as the fishermen opted for the smaller, easily handled nobbies. Nevertheless the boats still needed servicing in the same way as before, and by the outbreak of war, Teare

Peel harbour stuffed full of steam drifters.

and Sons had shares in some 24 fishing boats as well as 11 trading schooners.

The company was lucky to have survived from the Dumbells Bank failure of 1900, the bank being an important one on the Island. For many in the fishing industry it meant financial disaster and their boats were either sold to Ireland which was building up its fleet with financial assistance, or simply left to rot. The Peel (I.O.M.) Fishing Company, founded in 1892 to act as a sort of cooperative for the fishermen when selling their herring, was one of the victims of the slow-down, and was wound up the same year. Many fishermen left the industry, some even leaving the Island to work elsewhere. Ironically this clashed with an increase in the amount of herring with Port St. Mary benefitting from this by the building of a curing station in 1909. For those Peel fishers still in business in a severely depleted fleet, it was a matter of hit and miss. However, motorisation came in 1910 in the form of a Dan engine fitted into a nobby though, by the time of war in 1914, there were only 57 vessels in the Manx herring fleet. During this period the two steam drifters – *Manx Princess* and *Manx Bride* – were launched.

The steam trawler *Brothers*, BF149, entering Peel.

ENTERING HARBOUR PEEL I O M

Postcard view of the herring season at Peel.

Scottish ringers landing into Peel.

The fleet on the breakwater in 1954.

Between the wars more change brought about the demise of the last nickey in 1927, the first ring-netters from the Clyde in 1935, and the last motorised nobby in 1945. Ring netting was a form of fishing, originating from Loch Fyne, whereby a net is spread around a shoal using two boats (ringers), and the bottom rope tightened to form a bag, from which the herring can then be brought alongside, between both boats, and be brailed aboard using dip-nets. It was found to be a very effective way of fishing. The more modern ringer, either canoe or cruiser sterned, had been universally adopted. But as the 1960s approached, more stormy times lay ahead for the Peel herring fishermen.

A Night at the Herring

There are numerous reports written in the nineteenth
century from visitors to the Island who went out to
experience a night at the herring. My chosen scribe is the
Reverend A. M. Fosbrooke BA who was the curate of Stoke-
on-Trent and who submitted his 'A Night in a Herring Boat' to
be published in Church Monthly around the turn of the
twentieth century.[8]

    The good Reverend sailed out from Port Erin one breezy
afternoon at three o'clock aboard the *Puffin*, along with seven
fishermen. He witnessed a beautiful sunset at around 8pm
on that August evening. Once they were midway between the
Manx coast and that of the Mourne Mountains, and seeing 'a
large number of puffins and other birds' flying about, they
decided to shoot the nets. These natural appearances, as they
were referred to, suggest to the fishermen that there are

Golden Stream,
PL146, sailing out of
Peel harbour.

shoals of herring about that the birds were feeding upon. With the sails lowered except for a small jib – which itself suggests a nobby rig – to keep a bit of forward motion to the boat, the nets were cast out. His description of shooting is worthy of repeating.

One man connects the net to the spring-back, the long strong rope from which hang the long thin ropes, called legs, which are attached to the top of the net. 'Let me try and explain', he writes, 'the nature and position of the net as it lies in the water. On the surface there are large cork floats about every ten yards, from these hang down thin ropes, called the "straps", about nine feet long, which are fastened to the spring-back mentioned above; from this, again, having thin ropes, called the "legs", about twelve feet long; these are fastened to the rope along the top of the net, which is called the "back", and the net itself, weighted at the bottom to keep it perpendicular, is about thirty feet deep; so that from the surface of the water to the top of the net is about twenty-one feet, to the bottom of the net fifty-one feet. The length of the net is about one mile, or sometimes longer than that.'

Once the net had been shot, then the mast was lowered 'by an ingenious device', and the mizzen sail set to keep the vessel's head to the wind as she rode to the nets. By that time it was dark so a light was lit and one man set to stay on watch.

Once down below, 'before we lay down to rest in the

Illustration of a drift-net.

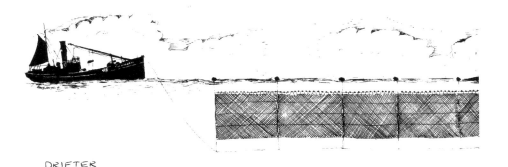

DRIFTER

The nobby *Ida*, PL270, leaving Peel for a night at the herring.

small cabin an impressive little incident occurred. An evening hymn was sung, and a prayer offered by one of the men (several of them take it in turns), commending themselves and their loved ones to the care of our Heavenly Father, and asking him to preserve to them the produce of the seas. It was the prayer of a rugged, uncultivated nature, and perhaps, in some respects, would seem offensive to refined minds; but it came from the heart, and so was undoubtedly well pleasing in His sight.' This was a common thing aboard Manx boats, and indeed, other boats around the UK coast. Yet it's hard to imagine seven rugged fishers kneeling down in the cramped accommodation, and recounting prayers.

Fosbrooke seemed to consider his fellow crew as hard working noble characters, 'temperate in their habits, pure in their conversation, and godly in their lives'. In this case there was no alcohol aboard. Traditionally, it is said, that a bottle of rum would be opened up once out of port, and served to each crew member in a measured horn that had been handed down through the generations. Temperance had, by then,

The Peel fleet of nobbies.

generally seen an end to the habit of drinking at sea.

The cabin was 'three yards long by two yards wide', and pretty stifling hot with the stove going and the motion of the boat in the rough sea which he wrote was 'conducive to sea-sickness'. At some point somebody must have checked the nets to see if the herring were 'creeping on', as they called it, by hauling in the first section or two of net. Then at three o'clock, the crew were roused from their slumbers and the process of hauling the net begun. He regarded this as the most interesting part of the proceedings.

'Two men work at the winch, hauling in the spring-back. The boat is thus gradually drawn along by the weight of the net. Another man unfastens the cords connecting the spring-back to the net; two others haul in the net, and set free the fish; one arranges the net in order in the hold as it comes in; another coils up the spring-back in another part of the hold; so that seven men are all really required for the work.' This hauling took over an hour, after which the mast was raised, sails set and the boat headed home.

The haul was not good. Only some 400 herrings though he noted that the fishing hadn't been good for the last four or five years. Before that a hundred mease (about 60,000 fish) was a common catch, the boat loaded to capacity.

Breakfast was coffee, bread and butter and fresh herring and, with a good wind they watched the sunrise over the Manx hills and were then back in Port Erin for 8 am.

Once home, the fish would normally have been checked by a buyer and a price agreed over a slug of rum. A coin also passed from buyer to skipper as part of the agreement and this was called the *eearlys* or *earnest*. With a catch this small it would probably be pretty pointless unless the buyer was desperate for fish!

Herring were measured by the mease. The cran (37½ Imperial gallons, on average 1200 fish) used to be the measure as regulated by the Act of Tynwald 1871, but they reverted to the mease. A Long Hundred was 124 fish and was counted out thus. Fish are thrown into a box in threes called a warp. Ten warps and one tally is thrown as well. After four tallies, you have 40 warps and 4 tallies which equals 124 fish. A mease was five Long Hundreds, i.e. 620 fish. In 1908 the cran measure was adopted as the stipulated measure for herring in England and Wales, and the Isle of Man followed suit. Then a standard quarter-cran basket was the accepted method of measuring and landing herrings.

Nobbies and a steam trawler alongside Peel breakwater c.1900.

Manx Belle, PL62, at Ramsey.

Frey, CT137, with her dredges down. (photo courtesy of Darren Purves)

Transition

The 1960s: and not for the first time did the Manx fishers
see a decline in herring catches. In Peel dwindling numbers
of boats set sail for the nightly drift-netting. Brian Cain
remembers spending eighteen months on the Peel-
registered *Manx Belle*, but when the owner went bankrupt
he joined *Senora* and that their last season was in 1967.

"I think it was 1967. Time when I put a new roof on my
house. We were one of the last, if not the last, at Peel with
the drift-net. Port Erin survived maybe a couple of years
more. We'd set small nets in spring, probably a mile long
they were. Then in July we'd get a bigger mesh so that the
smaller stuff could escape. It was the ringers, you know.
They did it in. Boats from the Clyde. They were good at it.
Then the big boats with their huge purse-seines. They were
even worse," he recalls, a glimmer of sadness in his eyes. "I
remember the ringers coming in, absolutely gunwaled up
with herring. Every size they'd take whereas our drift-nets
let the smaller stuff through. It all went for fish meal and
Peel stank."

There were originally a very few Manx boats that ring-
netted but generally it was left to the Scottish boats that
came down from Campbeltown and Tarbert, and the east
side of the Clyde. Beautiful varnished ringers which were
perfected in the art of catching herring. However, according
to the Manx Herring Fishery Report of 1965, there were only
seven ring-netters that year, six being Scottish and the other
from Northern Ireland. Out of the 34 boats that fished the
herring that year, seven were Manx, 21 Irish and the six
Scottish ringers. Only 2 Manx boats were drifting whilst five
trawled. Catches increased considerably in 1965 compared
to the previous year which had been regarded as disastrous.
A total of 25,797 crans landed in total as against 5,615 in
1964. Of this only 6,358 was landed into the Island where

Opposite: Scallops!

the price was lower than elsewhere. Over half of this was kippered, the rest being processed as fish meal, pickle-cured or frozen.

"Then I went on the smaller boat *Lil Marina*, PL21, with Billy Mac and I was with him for eighteen years. Scalloping we were, and the queenies. We could fish queenies all year round if we wanted when we started. They were an unknown quantity. Shovelling out the scallops to throw over from huge piles of queenies. I remember we got thirty-three shillings a bag, and big bags they were." He offers his hand about three feet off the floor. Bags as big as those the scallops are brought ashore in now.

"We'd get fifty bags quickly, and be home by lunchtime," he added. "We used a sort of dredge, half trawl, half dredge I guess. There's a beam about eight feet long with rubber discs and chains to dislodge the queenies and netting behind to catch them. Very basic in the early days. All the queenies were sent to Kirkcudbright in their first years and then the merchants began to come to Peel to start up here."

I asked about scallops.

"Yes, scallops were unrestricted at the time too and again there was a massive concentration of fishing until restrictions were put in place. I remember we lost the gear one year, snagged on a rock just off here," he said, pointing out of his living room window over the bay near Niarbyl. "A diver went down but he couldn't find it. Said he could see where the teeth had left grooves in the rock though!"

What about the prawns?

"We did a bit of prawns, not much. They are mostly over towards the Irish coast." Indeed they were now and I remember being shown a website where all the prawn boats are tracked, and from this it was obvious that the main trawling grounds were in the deeper water between the Island and the Irish coast.

So, the 1960s: a period of transition.

A dredgeful of scallops!

King and Queen Scallops

Pecten maximus and *Chlamys opercularis*

Scallops are probably my most favourite seafood, just surpassing mussels which I love and eat often. Scallops are more scarce in Britain as the majority of the UK catch seems to be exported. That which is left tends to fetch high prices on the fish counters. Queenies I've only ever bought in the Isle of Man, and not seen fresh on the UK mainland.

Scallops (king scallops) and queenies (queen scallops) both have round shells although the queenie is approximately a quarter the size of the scallop at marketable size. The scallop has one flat and one rounded shell and it tends to lie in hollows in the seabed, curved side down with the top flat shell almost level with the seabed so that it can have a thin layer of silt covering it. The queenie, on the other hand, sits onto the seabed and does not recess itself into it. In the Irish Sea they both occur in depths between about 10 to 25 fathoms, and they like strong currents that bring them food to filter in the form of plankton and bacteria.

Unloading bags of scallops at Peel in 2015. (photo courtesy of Mike Craine)

Scallops can live up to 20 years whilst queenies survive for about eight years. Manx Scallops have a minimum landing size of 110mm across the shell and take several years to reach this age. Queenies grow much quicker and are landed when at least 55mm, a size they can reach in under two years.

Both species swim by quickly clapping their shells, and queenies are more active in this action. Indeed, they can swim fair distances according to some reports from fishermen who say they've seen them swimming near the surface.

Scallops have been fished commercially in the Isle of Man since 1937. However today's scallop dredging is very different

Opposite top:
Frey, CT137.
(photo courtesy of Darren Purves)

Opposite bottom:
The scalloper/trawler *Marida*, DO37, built by the yard of James N. Miller & Sons of St. Monans, Scotland, in 1968, alongside in Douglas in January 2018.)

Ramsey quayside with whelk pots and queenie trawls in January 2018.

A queenie trawl aboard the trawler *Venture Again*, PL39, alongside at Ramsey in August 2017.

Queenie trawler *Sarah Lena*, CT 18, coming into Port St Mary. (photo courtesy of Mike Craine)

to when it started back in the earlier part of the twentieth century when a visiting Irishman alerted the Manx to the dense shoals of scallops off Bradda Head. The Island has rich grounds in its territorial waters that extend to 12 miles out. Inshore fishing is classed as being within the 3 mile limit.

Although queen scallops had been caught by fishermen dredging for scallops since then, they were discarded, being considered inferior to the king scallop and only fit for baiting long-lines. How things change so that, when a market for frozen queenie meat was discovered in the USA, almost overnight, it became a profitable fishery. That was in 1969.

Although they are now fished in the summer months between July and September, outside of the scallop season (1st November to 31st May) and have been for many years, to begin with they were fished all year round. There are stories of boats catching 350 bags a go and being home before the shops close. These they caught using an adapted dredge (the Blake

Queenie trawler *Maureen Patricia*, CT76, entering Port St. Mary to unload her bags of queenies in August 2017.

dredge) which was designed by Manx blacksmiths to run over the seabed. Queenies tended to swim upwards and this was designed to catch them as they did so, discarding broken shells and stones. It was a bit like a beam trawl, about eight feet long, with two or three runners and chain ground rope instead of blades and netting at the back with a mesh capable of allowing undersize queenie to fall out. Today's trawls run on bobbins, or rockhoppers, on the foot rope though some still use dredges. Basically it all depends on the type of ground they are working over, and the horsepower of the boat.

Although queenies were fished along the west coast of the Isle of Man in the early days, and discarded during scallop dredging, the main grounds today are to the north of the island, stretching over to Morecambe Bay and almost as far south as Liverpool. Today when boats are fishing queenies, they have to discard the scallops. A reversal of fortunes from the days when they happily discarded queenies when dredging for scallops!

The 107ft queenie dredger *Mattanja*, TN36, now called *Albatross*, BA 88, with its 18 dredges per side leaving Douglas. (photo courtesy of Mike Craine)

A Day at the Scallops

Five a.m. and it's pitch black save for a faint starry night that seems to hover overhead but not share any light. The gales have departed and the forecast gives a brief window before the next arrives tonight. As arranged, I donned winter gear and arrived into the brighter lights of Peel and was about to cross the river over the new footbridge when the first of the fleet cast off just as the bridge opened. I looked at my watch and I could see across that the lights of the *Silver Viking* had been awakened. I had five minutes to reach her: the only option was to run right around the harbour, to the road bridge. Thus I did arrive just as the lines were being slackened, skipper Alex Ironside asking whether the figure he'd seen running down the other side of there harbour was I. "Yep," I replied. "There's nothing like an early morning jog!" "We'd have picked you up off the breakwater," replied Alex. No gruff response then, just a very friendly welcome with added smiling nods from his two crew Kelvin (nickname Elvis) and Alex (nickname Dobag). This was going to be a good day I decided.

The king scallop fleet at the start of the scallop fishing on Nov 2nd 2017 with some 50 boats ready to start fishing. (photo courtesy of Mike Craine)

We manoeuvred out from the berth almost immediately and I climbed into the wheelhouse as we passed the footbridge and the engine pitch increased as we motored past the breakwater. The vessel began to roll in the northerly swell as we surged out into the total blackness ahead. "She's quite shallow in the draft," said Alex in reply to my silent thoughts. "Only two metres, a bit over six feet."

The 48ft-long *Silver Viking*, PL19, was built in Eyemouth in 1973 and was purchased by Alex's father in 1998 from Mallaig and five years ago he passed it over to Alex. He'd been

The first dredges come up in darkness.

Sunrise over Mull Hill.

at the scallops ever since, when the weather allowed. From the 1st November through to the end of May, they'd be out when the weather allowed.

"Haven't been out since the beginning of January. We had about six clear days early on and nothing but gales since. Today's the first gap. Gales again tonight, all weekend. Might get out next Tuesday again." Today was the 26th January. That would be a maximum of eight days out of 31. Could be worse, as it has been some winters when nature bombards the Island with wind and rain for months. But that's the nature of fishing anywhere. And given that the Isle of Man is a small island in the middle of the Irish Sea, open to the elements from all directions, maybe eight days in January is good!

"It's good to give the boat a run. Charge the batteries. Earn some money. Some of the fleet will sail, others won't," he replied to my query about the lack of boats around us. Two had left just before, one sailing away up to the north of the island, the other on a similar heading to us as we altered course to the south. We were off to the 'back of the hill' scallop ground between Peel and the Calf.

Fishing can continue seven days a

Hauling the dredges up to the surface.

51

The dredges coming up and resting on the bulwarks.

week between the hours of six a.m. and six p.m. Satellite tracking ensures compliance and Alex had already logged into the fisheries site to say we'd left. Five to six and the boys began to get the gear ready to drop. One minute to and the winch starts letting out the gear both sides. As six o'clock dawned, dredging commenced. There's no need to waste time here. But start early and woe betide the outcome. One skipper was fined £5000 for commencing 15 minutes early.

So scallop dredging has become one of the most regulated fisheries. For the Isle of Man, it earns some £12 million annually. But for the fishermen, the general consensus is that the government doesn't really care. Some 90 boats are licensed to fish the scallops yet only 37 of the boats are Manx boats, representing 35% of those scalloping in 2017 figures. In other words the Northern Irish (27%), Scots (23%), English (13%) and Welsh (2%) boats simply come and help themselves and rarely land on the Island. However, it should be pointed out that Manx boats have some 90% of the inshore 0-3mile sector.

"They're robbing us of our livelihoods," I heard from more than one quarter. "The Scots come in their bigger boats and dredge and take far more than they are meant to. Nobody checks them. The authorities turn a blind eye." That was a common cry. At that moment the 'scallop wars' were on, in that there was pressure upon the Scots to declare their genuine catches. Story was that they were bagging far more than the 20 bags and the authorities in Kirkcudbright were turning a blind eye. Sadly, as we listened on the radio, the Manx had given in with an agreement

Emptying each dredge in turn.

Preparing to drop the dredge after emptying, skipper on the right controlling the winch.

that they would withdraw licences from any Scottish boat found to be understating their catches. The general opinion was that the Manx government had capitulated.

"But what about the fisheries protection boat?" I asked. The *Barrule* I'd seen tied up in Douglas. Alex laughed.

"That has no skipper. He walked off and now they can't get anyone else so it doesn't go out. The Scots' boats know this. It's a joke. Someone told me they've 80 people in the fisheries office but whenever I put my forms into the letterbox at Peel it's always full. No one to empty it."

But you can't blame these guys for thinking the government isn't behind them. When I look at today's fishing compared to it when the herring was king it's a mere blink. There's scallops now, with queenies in July, August and September. Then there's a few boats potting for crabs and lobsters. Nothing else. The herring quota was sold off by the government several years back when the price plummeted and nobody wanted to fish them. Last year two Northern Irish boats swept the whole 3500 ton quota up in a matter of a week or so. Likewise there's no other quota for prawns and not much whitefish anyway!

Back to the practicalities. We dredged along a southerly route about one and a half to two miles off the coast for an hour and twenty minutes. Then hauling commenced. Working in about 30 fathoms, there was 70 fathoms of tow wire out and after about a minute the upper rings of the gear appear. The hook of the metal block fed from a rope is attached and the steel tow line slackened as the rope line takes the strain from the gantry which allows the gear to swing forward. This is hauled in and the teeth of the dredges rest on the gunwale, the bags of the dredges hanging over the side. Each one is then lifted using another strop and emptied onto the deck. We are using five dredges per side, ten in all. Once one side is emptied, the gear is dropped back into the water and the tow rope taking the strain. The same is repeated the other side and before long both sets of dredges are down and once again the winch runs out, setting the dredges back onto the seabed. The whole process takes ten minutes which explains why we dredged for one hour, twenty minutes. One and a half hours between the start of each run gives the possibility of eight runs between the permitted hours of work.

Once the dredges have been shot, sorting the catch begins.

This dredge produced two bags of scallops, each carefully sorted through by Kelvin on one side and Alex the other. Small scallops were discarded and large put into a basket. Both of them used a stainless steel gauge to decide if the scallop was of the permitted landing size of 110mm across the shell at the widest point. What amazed me was the lack of stuff in the rubbish of all the six dredge runs we did throughout the day. Small scallops put back to grow, lots of starfish that eat scallops and thus are regarded as pests, empty scallops shells, the odd rock, one small mackerel and a tiny monkfish, hardly any weed and not much else. Reports of dredging ripping up coral reefs and tearing through fields of seaweed are obviously wrong here. The seabed is sandy and flat, perfect for the scallops to breed, which is why we are here. I remember someone likening it to ploughing the land, but here the dredge merely tickles the surface rather than digging in.

Alex explained the workings of the dredges which are quite complicated in design. They are metal framed, fixed to the long towbar that has 16inch rubber wheels on both ends. This runs along the seabed with the five dredges below. The metal teeth of the dredges are set with springs either side so that they vibrate – he described it as chattering – and hence flick the scallops up from their home in the sand. The size of teeth depends on the firmness of the seabed and whether its sand or gravel. Furthermore the springs can be tightened or loosened to suit the conditions, all this being done prior to sailing. The bags consist of metal rings on the bottom and

Using the gauge to check that no undersize scallops are landed.

rope netting above. Cost of a new dredge: £900. That amazed me but when you consider the tempered steel, the stainless steel rings, the teeth at £120 a set and the rest, I guess it quickly added up. Teeth sometimes only last a few days of work and have to be welded onto the bar ashore. Springs can snap easily but only cost £4.50 each! In all, a new set of dredges all round, a new tow bar and the rest would cost almost £15,000. Add that to the cost of fuel (approx £170 a day), and general upkeep of the boat, then one sees that £115 a bag of scallops from the dealer is not unreasonable. £1700 for the day, less 15% each to Kelvin and Alex (approx £500) leaves £1200 to the boat and skipper. Pay the fuel and then break a dredge and it's gone!

So once the sorting was completed and the detritus chucked over the side, the baskets of scallops were put into the white bags supplied by the merchant in Peel, proudly displaying 'Isle of Man scallops' and the name of the boat. Then the lads disappeared down below to make coffee and, I suspect, have a quick nap. By the time the dredges appeared over the side for the second time, the sun was throwing out rays from behind Bradda Head, the sky blue and cloudless.

Bagging the scallops.

The sloppiness of the sea had calmed and we were certainly heading into a beautiful winter's day. This dredge realised two and a quarter bags once completed. I remarked to Alex how well his two lads worked together, each knowing exactly what to do and then, as they worked together bagging, each laughing and smiling.

"See them after eight consecutive days and they aren't!" he said. "But, yes, they've been with me for two years. Both their first times and so they've learned with me. But they are mates too, go on holiday together. The boat's booked into the slipway at Maryport for ten days in June when there's nothing

Unloading alongside the quay at Peel.

to fish, for repainting and a bit of welding here and there, and they've booked a holiday then. 'We are fishermen', they said, 'not painters and decorators', so the yard will do the work. I'll sail her over and come back. That'll end up costing ten or twelve thousand."

By midday the sea had calmed and the wind gone round to the west. Although the sun was warm and the sky continued to stay blue, on the horizon a haze denoted a change coming. By the time we were hauling in our last shot, the sky was overcast and the wind had backed more to the south west and we all knew that before long the wind would increase, forecast to be Force 7. Our last dredge – longer than the previous – realised three and a half bags, taking the tally up to the required 15. When I asked what happens if they'd been more, Alex remarked that it was only really a gentleman's agreement. It's 20 really, as we can fish outside the three-mile limit, but we've all agreed to this inside the 3-mile. 15 is enough to secure the future of the fishery. We've probably shot ourselves in the foot as the Scots and Irish don't really care. See some of the boats that have up to 18 dredges per side and imagine how much they dredge. They're the ones that are damaging both the industry and the seabed."

"It's the same with the lobster and crab boats. We work together. We know where they put their pots so we do not dredge there. Likewise they know where we want to dredge so they never put their pots down there."

"How many boats pot?"

'Two or three from Peel, depending on the time of year. In winter the pots are further out but there's the constant danger of losing them in the gales. But what else is there for us? No whitefish quota, no herring quota. Just scallops, queenies and lobsters and crabs!"

The one bonanza they have is a day's dredging for scallops in Ramsey bay. It's a marine reserve in that the scallops are left. But in late December each Manx boat is allowed one day's fishing where they catch scallops much larger. For the fishermen the prize is that less scallops fill the bag and the price per bag is higher. Smaller scallops are left behind. A nice little earner before Christmas, they say. Better than empty shells littering the seabed, they say!

Back in Peel the bags are hauled up onto the Caley Fisheries lorry to be shucked and exported to Europe and beyond, and the boat tied up. The tide is too low to get into the harbour so Alex is happy to leave her on the breakwater. Two other boats come in and unload. We clamber up the ladder onto the breakwater and walk past the castle, and I note the footbridge is open as the scalloper *Regal Star* enters. But by the time we reach it, the bridge is once again in place and the crew are able to cross. No running round the long way for them. We say our farewells, hands shake all round, and it seems like days since the early morning.

And the saddest thing I read in the local newspaper later that evening. A report on the concentration of scallop dredging just out showed, in 2008, the area around the Isle of Man as having less than 800 days dredging, the lowest around the whole of the UK. By 2016 the opposite was the case with the same waters having the greatest concentration of somewhere between 3,200 and 4,011 dredging days. With these sorts of levels of dredging, I wonder just how long can the scallop fishing survive.

Silver Viking, PL19, coming back into Peel and, yes, that's me at the window! (photo courtesy of Darren Purves)

Longshore Fishing in the Late 19th Century

It's too easy to think of fishing as a full-time job, justifiably so because these days it generally is. But go back a century or more it was more often seasonal, dependent on the harvest from the land and, as ever, the weather. Living on the edge between land and sea dictated working the land when nature demanded and using the sea when time allowed.

Given that the Manx inhabitants seldom lived more than a few miles from the sea, there was a flourishing coastal fishery off any probable beach landing up to, say, the late nineteenth century. Identifying those beach landings today is not without its problems but it is easy to see that fishing, as a means of survival, was practised from the following beaches:

Starting in the north and travelling clockwise, we've identified Phurt, Port Lewaigue, Port Mooar, Port Cornaa, Garwick, Port Groudle, Keristal, Port Soderick, Port Grenaugh, Fleshwick Bay, Niarbyl, Glen Maye, Kirk Michael and Lhen.

The inshore boat – the *baulk* yawl – was heavily influenced by Norse boatbuilding traditions.

Boats at Garwick. Such beaches had been the bases for inshore fishermen for generations.

Before harbours were built, the same could be said for Laxey, Derby Haven, Castletown and Port Erin. On purpose I've not mentioned Ramsey, Douglas, Port St. Mary and Peel though, before they became major fishing harbours, fishing was undoubtedly practised off the beaches long before harbour facilities were built. In Peel it is said that there were 80-90 long-line fishers which had increased to 150 within three years.[9] Long-lines, after all, were used in Viking times (and probably much earlier) as attested by the hooks found in Viking graves on the Island.

Back in the eighteenth century the 'baulk yawl' or *balc yawl* was said to be the favoured boat, 'baulk' meaning long-line. This appears to simply have been a smaller version of the herring 'scowte', rigged in a similar way with a single squaresail. In Ballaugh in 1774, there were six small yawls employed in catching grey fish and crewed generally by old men.[10]

The boats were named after the part of the coast they worked from, or the person that owned the boat. Hence, around Lhen (written as Lhane in the notes) in the northwest,

The same Garwick beach. Note B24 again from the previous photo. By this time most of the boats would be taking trippers around the bay.

we find fishermen John Lace referring to 'Foawr's yawl' standing outside the house of the Faragher's, a crofter family, or 'Lhoob yawls' because that part of the coast from Cronk y Bing to the limekiln was called the Lhoob[11]. The descriptions in these notes for this northern area of the Island give a good insight into the workings of longshore fishing in the last decades of the nineteenth century and can be deemed fairly typical around the coast. Fifteen vessels were said to be fishing this part of the coast in the 1860s, between Jurby Head and Blue Point to the north.

Small inshore boats at Ramsey in 1938, photographer unknown. These were typical of the boats working long-lines and setting nets inshore.

Fish was said to be in abundant supply along this coast, as it was all around the Island. They used to say that 'one could put the pot on the fire and go to the shore with no doubt of getting a fish to put into it'.

The men long-lined and occasionally trawled. The favoured catch was generally referred to as greyfish (cod, haddock etc) though there were skate banks off Jurby as well as copious amounts of sandeel, locally called *gibbin*. These were sometimes scraped up off the soft sand using a blunt sickle made locally. When cured and dried they were called *dhollans* and became pretty crispy after being fried. The story went that one man went to work in Liverpool, taking dried *gibbin* with him, and whilst eating these at work one of his mates remarked, 'Look at the Manx devil eating horseshoe nails'.

The long-lines, of which they generally set four to six lines, were weighted with stones and baited with whelks, locally called *bucks* or *muttlags*. The lines consisted of 20 coils of line 26 fathoms long (1440 yards in total) with a lighter line every five or six yards to which a hook is attached. Thus an average line had 260 hooks. They were made up by the fishermen and each took a day to make. Cost was £2 in about 1880. The whelk pots were wicker and made locally, being themselves baited with fish heads or any fish they didn't eat, even salt herring. The pots were weighted with stones and marked with a stick of corks that only floated at slack water.

Before the advent of electronic plotters and the like on fishing vessels, fishermen used landmarks to know where to fish. This was true for herring fishing up to the mid-twentieth century. For these northern fishers their landmarks – a house maybe, or Jurby church or hill – had the Manx name *aahley*, thus *aahley vooar* or *aahley veg*.

The catch was mostly sold in the locality by cart, though sometimes, as the catches decreased in the latter part of the century and the number of boats fishing reduced, the catch was taken to Ramsey and sold to fish dealers. In 1870 there were seven yawls with sails at Lhen. Boat numbers then decreased to two by the turn of the century, one at Lhoob and the other at Gob Gorrym. Trawling was generally blamed for the scarcity of fish though locally some blamed Ayre farmer Tommy Cormode who took a horse and harrow

Mrs Kinnin (on right in white apron). She was a well known fish salesperson in Ramsey and is seen here with a good catch of herring on the quayside. (photo courtesy of Joe Pennington)

The beach at Keristal. Note how the fishermen cleared a path in so that their boats wouldn't ground on the rough stones and rocks. The dog-leg is to prevent the build up of surf on that part of the beach. (photo courtesy of Mike Craine)

to the beach and scraped up all the *gibbon* which was never seen again. Take away the food of the fish and don't be surprised that the fish themselves disappear!

The boats in the late nineteenth century had changed over to a lug rig in the same way as the bigger boats had, and were 'fifteen to eighteen feet long with four oars and a lug sail'. Some had a small transom stern. They were drawn up the beach on pieces of wood beneath the keel called *stuggyrs* covered in wet wrack, a local coarse brown seaweed. At low water the boats would be left anchored out and brought in once the tide had flooded. Often built by the men themselves on the beaches, one report notes the 'Gob Gorrym Shipyard in Andreas as being a producer of baulk yawls and partly

Boats off Castletown (seen in the background). The small boat is a baulk yawl and the other a dandy-rigged lugger with another cutter-rigged behind the one in the fore lowering the mainsail.

65

Niarbyl beach with boats. This has a magnetism that has attracted visitors and locals alike.

decked boats'.[12] A letter from William Cubbon to Cyril Paton in 1936 mentions a small boatbuilder's yard at the mouth of the Lhen.[13] As fishing declined, and tourism increased, some boats survived by taking trippers out for a run around the bay.

As the local fishing declined, the men went off with the larger boats to the Whitehaven cod fishing in early spring, the Kinsale mackerel fishery and the summer and autumn herring. An example was Skipper Hastie of Peel who hove his nickey off Lhen to pick up his crew. His small boat brought out several men, along with their bedding, clothing, lines and bait pots, thus saving them carrying all their gear to Peel.

In the north, fishing became centred on Ramsey where boats sailed out for the banks for mackerel using hand lines. A particular type of boat developed for this, clinker-built and open at first, becoming half-decked and somewhat similar in design to boats fishing off the Cumbrian, Lancashire and North Wales coasts. These were counter sterned, quite low in the freeboard and cutter rigged.

In the south, at Niarbyl for example, where there were said once to be a hundred men fishing the bay that stretched from Dalby Point to Bradda Head, including Fleshwick Bay, the remains of lead in the rocks is said to be where holes were drilled out for mooring rings for the small boats. At Niarbyl, a channel was dug out for the small herring rowboats to return after a night's drifting. However, much of the clearing was for the smuggling, especially the paths down to the coast. For example, according to Alan Kermode, the path going down to Hastel took a considerable amount of digging out and that there would have to be a good reason. As there was no mining there, smuggling he assumes was the reason. For crofter/fishermen these paths became very useful. Billy the Tweet was known for setting a long-line at Niarbyl that consisted of 40 hooks.[14]

Lobster pots at Niarbyl in August 2017.

Today the beaches of the Island are somewhat quieter although there can be found some activity on the water during the summer. More likely they are the domain of dog walkers and anglers, and I noted on many beaches notices informing anglers that only one bass of a certain size can be landed each day. But fish there still is, and the Port Erin annual herring seine of the beach attracts equal amounts of local interest and fish!

Nickeys alongside Port St. Mary. The boat in the centre is *Zetland*, CT97, and she ended up being sold to Southern Ireland in 1913. CT stands for Castletown.

The nickey *Golden Plover*, PL77, built in 1881 and owned by 'J. Teare and others'.

The nobby *Gladys*, PL61, built in 1901 by Neakle & Watterson.

Scowtes to Nobbies – the Evolution of Manx Sailing Fishing Craft

Throughout history man has found that his watercraft evolve through usage and availability of materials, from early log boats through to the modern fibreglass and steel craft of today. Fishing craft are no exception, and documented evidence shows that the types of craft used are influenced by various factors such as the place they work from, the seas around them, the method of fishing and tradition passed down through the generations. Change is brought about by innovation by either fisherman or boatbuilder.

For Manx craft, the earliest documented are the Viking-type herring *scowtes*, single masted, square-sailed vessels used specifically to chase the herring shoals. These were variants on the Icelandic *skuta* which were fast vessels carrying sails and

Gladys coming into Peel harbour in August 2017 after a complete rebuild in Falmouth where she is owned and kept by Charlotte Whyte.

White Heather, PL5, sailing off Peel in about 2010 with the traditional nobby rig of dipping lug mainsail and standing lug mizzen.

oars. Like the generic Viking longship, these had considerable sheer forward, curved stems and sternposts and were open craft. Lengths of their keels – the normal way of measuring craft in days gone by – were between 20 and 24ft, giving them an overall length of up to 28 feet. They were clinker built (planks overlapping instead of edge-to as in 'carvel') and the cost of a boat then was about £75. It was a fleet of these *scowtes* that sailed out to the nightly herring fishing that fateful evening of 20th September 1787. (see page 14)

Gien Mie, FD5, built as PL83 by Neakle and Watterson in 1913, working from Fleetwood where she was transferred to in 1954. She was dismantled in 1996.

With the fleet severely diminished, there was an urgency to find and develop new craft. Smacks were already transporting goods around the coasts as were wherry-rigged vessels. A mixture of these were used to fish, and the larger half-decked smacks, often called *dagons*, soon out-performed the open wherries, and thus more were built specifically for fishing. These gave a modicum of shelter in the forepeak, with onboard sleeping and cooking facilities and increased safety through being partially decked over. By 1800 it was reported that the Manx fleet reached its highest numbers with some 600 boats from local owners.

In 1823 the first Scottish and Cornish boats appeared and fishing was so successful that they began to return year after year. The Cornishmen came in their powerful drivers – lug-rigged with two masts. They then tended to ride to their drift-nets with the mainmast lowered and only the mizzen sail set.

The Manxmen saw the advantage and quickly adapted their own vessels by shortening the main boom and

Two long-liners alongside at Ramsey in 1938. Although often referred to as half-deckers, they were generally decked over with a long cockpit, with the added comfort of a small deckhouse and forepeak 'cuddy'.

Deck view of the 38ft long-liner *Master Frank*, RY85. Having no deckhouse, the long cockpit in the traditional 1895 format is perhaps more obvious to these boats being classed as half-deckers. The counter stern is much squarer than *Caribou*'s in the previous photo though there are many similarities to the Morecambe Bay nobbies just across the water. (photo courtesy of Mike Craine)

stepping a jigger mizzen mast to convert to a dandy rig of gaff mainsail and lug mizzen. They also stepped the mainmast in a tabernacle so they, too, could lower it when lying to their nets.

These became known as the *Manx luggers* and between 1840 and 1860 almost the entire fleet was thus rigged. In 1848 the price of such a vessel was £155 for a 40ft vessel. However, as boatbuilding techniques improved, sizes increased to around 55ft and the largest were entirely decked over.

By the 1860s the Cornish had perfected their luggers and were visiting the Island in numbers. The Manxmen, instead of building the dandy-rigged craft began to copy the Cornish boats in hull shape and rig. Because a large proportion of Cornish fishermen were named Nicholas, so it is said, they termed their new boats *nickeys*! At first they bought in

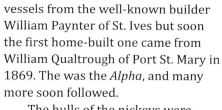

vessels from the well-known builder William Paynter of St. Ives but soon the first home-built one came from William Qualtrough of Port St. Mary in 1869. The was the *Alpha*, and many more soon followed.

The hulls of the nickeys were between 50 and 60ft. They had accommodation aft of the amidships fish hold, berths for eight crew and a stove. Forward of the fish hold was the net room and bosun's locker.

When sailing to the Kinsale mackerel fishing in March, they would commonly make the passage in forty-eight hours, a fast time even by today's standards. By 1881 there were 334 Manx boats taking part in the herring fishing, the largest number being registered in Peel and Castletown. So great had been the

demand for these vessels that, as well as the Manx yards building them, Paynter moved his works to Kilkeel from where he was able to supply both the Northern Irish and Manx demand. At that time the average cost of a nickey was at least £700 including sails and nets.

In 1884 the first of the new breed of ring-net boats appeared from the Clyde, heralding the first mutterings of another, and final, change in sailing fishing boat design. On the east side of the Clyde they called their vessels *nabbies* whilst to the west they were *Lochfyne skiffs*, both similar in design in that they were mostly half-deckers, had steeply-raked sternposts, upright stems and a sloping keel and one standing lugsail, which made them highly manoeuvrable, necessary when operating ring-nets. However the Manx fishers weren't generally taken by the ring-net as they generally believed this method would wipe out the shoals which were, in actuality, already in decline. Some years in

Master Frank heading out of Peel inner harbour in August 2017. Here the low counter stern and shallow freeboard reflect the need to work long-lines over the side whilst standing in the cockpit. Note the addition of the deckhouse in comparison to the previous photo.

the late 1870s had been very lean for the Peel fishers already. But an improvement in fortunes in the 1880s saw the Manxman copying the hull of the Scots boats although wholly decking over. These boats they called *nobbies* and were smaller than their predecessors at around 40 feet. The rig had two masts, both with lugsails as against the Scots' single masts. These continued to be built into the twentieth century. However, by the time of the outbreak of war in 1914, there were only 57 boats working from the Island, about 30 of which had been motorised. The advent of the internal combustion engine was about to change the face of fishing everywhere and the Isle of Man was no exception.

SURVIVING BOATS – A TESTAMENT TO THEIR LONGEVITY

We are lucky that several of these nobbies have survived. The oldest is *Gladys*, PL61, built in 1901 by Neakle and Watterson for local fisherman Thomas Cashen. Today she is based in Falmouth after a complete rebuild, and returned to the Island in August 2017 for the Peel Traditional Boat weekend.

White Heather, PL5, is still in Peel, built by the same builders

Postcard view of Port Erin in 1968.

in 1904 for G. Gaskill and now owned by Mike Clark who is busy replanking part of her as this is written. Like *Gladys*, she is lug rigged.

Vervine Blossom again hails from Neakle and Watterson, launched in 1910 and the first to have a canoe stern which, considering her engine wasn't fitted until 1912, shows innovation. The older straight sternpost didn't receive propeller apertures very well and the canoe stern shape thus evolved. *Gladys* had hers protruding out on the port side when fitted.

Aigh Vie, built 1917 with a 26hp Kelvin, has recently undergone a major refit in Ireland.

One other Manx boat built as a half-decker for cod fishing using long-lines on the short sharp waters northeast of the Island has survived. *Master Frank*, RY95, was built in 1896 by Clucas & Duggan for Whitehaven fish dealer Mr W. Shakley who named her after his son. However she returned to the Isle of Man a year later and fished commercially, generally for skate, until 1978. She now sails from Ramsey after a rebuild several years ago and is the oldest of the Manx craft. Sadly *Gien Mie*, PL83, built in 1913 by Neakle and Watterson as a long-liner, survived until 1996 when she was broken up after a collision with a larger vessel. Both these boats were similar in design to the Morecambe Bay nobbies – not to be confused with the Manx nobbies – which also worked in these waters and might be termed a parallel evolution.

Nickey *Golden Stream*. PL146, leaving Peel harbour.

Manx Princess.

Boatbuilding in the Isle of Man

The Isle of Man has a history of building seaworthy boats, and for the fishing industry, most boats were built on the island. Peel, especially, was foremost in boatbuilding, with vessels also being built for companies outside of the Island. However Peel didn't have a monopoly as William Qualtrough had his yard in Port St. Mary in the second half of the nineteenth century and is renowned for building the first nickey whilst Clucas & Duggan were in Ramsey at the turn of the century from where the oldest surviving Manx fishing boat originated. In more recent times the Ramsey Shipbuilding & Engineering Company in Ramsey built a couple of boats.

In Peel, small yards were established, one of the first referenced being Crellins in 1793. The yard survived many years as a receipt tells us that Robert Crellin built the fishing boat *Mona's Isle* in 1863. Another was Meyricks on the Promenade although they later moved to Peverill Road and supposedly launched one of their boats by lowering it down the headland because they were unable to bring it down Stanley Road! William Cottier's shipyard was in Market Street, and he produced many fine ships.[15] John and Caesar Corris's yard was opposite the White House pub and allegedly on launch day the men convened to the pub whilst the women hauled the boat down the road, thus the local saying 'The Peel girls are the boys'. They later moved down to the East Quay (they also owned the largest tannery on the Island). Graves Yard was also on the quay between the coal yard and the

Watson's boatyard across the river from Peel with nobby under build.

The nobby *Mairead* being built at Watson's yard c.1908 at about the time Thomas Watson went into liquidation.

Longhouse and they continued to build vessels until closure in 1897 and is reckoned to be the longest running Manx yard. The same family owned the rope factory out past where today's power station is, as well as the timber yard. Other names in the business were Tom Cowell and Tommy Gell.[16]

Thomas Watson, whose yard was on Mill Street, beyond where Moores's kipper yard is now, was probably the most successful in the last few decades of the nineteenth century, building many of the fishing boats up to the fleet's peak in 1878-79. As is often the case, he specialised in building yachts for gentlemen but fishing boats gave him his bread and butter, so to speak. Several luggers were built for Irish owners and one, the *Geraldine*, launched in 1884, was 47 feet in the keel and the cabins were lined in 'oak grains' and the berths 'commodious'. In 1887 business must have been good as he expanded into Coopers Mill which was across the river Neb. In 1890 he launched a nobby that was to long-line in winter and join the herring fleet in the summer and then another to work from Girvan and to participate in the

Another view of *Mairead* under construction. This is the yard on the far side of the river.

View down the river Neb with the footbridge and Watson's yard on the left and sawmill behind, and Watson's other yard across the river.

mackerel fishing. Steamers, schooners and yachts seem to have been launched in quick succession.

In June 1895, disaster struck in the form of a fire which destroyed a spar shed and gear, all of which was valued at £150 and which was uninsured. Times were lean for the fishermen though boats were still being launched and turned out every seven or eight weeks. In between, repairs kept things going but into the new century Thomas Watson got into financial difficulties which eventually led to the liquidation of the yard in 1908 and bankruptcy for Mr. Watson.

One name sticks in the mind when Peel fishing boats are mentioned. Messrs Neakle, Watterson and Cashen had already set up business in the Graves Yard when Watson's yard ceased to exist. Graves, as mentioned before, had closed in 1897. The first reference comes on March 13th 1897 when 'the new firm of Messrs Neakle, Watterson and Cashen, who had taken over Graves yard, had on March 10th 1897, launched a fishing boat. This was the *Minnie*, built for A.H.Bailey, Castle Street, Peel. The vessel, at 27.5 feet of keel, was to proceed to the Southern Ireland fishery'. Presumably this boat was already under construction when the yard changed hands. The 'and Cashen' was later dropped, thus becoming Neakle & Watterson.

In January 1898 'a splendid Nobby' was launched for the

Side launch of unknown boat.

Dublin Castle Congested Board. Another, *Ruby*, was launched at the end of March and yet another, *St. Joseph*, 712D, in September, both for the same Board. The latter was a large nobby with a keel length of 30ft. A note says that the Peel fishermen have no incentive to take an interest in fishing in the prevailing conditions. However the time span suggests they could build a nobby in three months.

The yard's first nobby for the local fleet was the 40ft *El Dorado* in June 1899. *Gladys* was launched in 1901. They built several yachts which seemed to perform really well and the yard gained excellent publicity in winning races. However, in 1904, there's a reference to the yard having four 'nobbys' on order, two for Dingle and two local.

White Heather was launched on Christmas Eve 1904 though not registered as PL5 until January 1905. Two years later they'd moved the yard to Mill Road opposite Watson's ailing yard, probably in preparation for their next project.

Thus Peel's first steam herring drifter, the 100ft *Manx Princess*, PL29 was launched on April 2nd 1908 for Mr C.F. Egner for whom they had previously built a yacht, the *Dolores*, two years earlier. The drifter had taken six months to build and then was towed to Govan to have the engine fitted by

The launch of *Cushag*, PL41, at Neakle & Watterson's yard in 1908. Little is known about this boat although she ended up in a creek at Annan Waterfoot in 1935.

Messrs McKee & Baxter. By July of that year she was ready to sail to the Shetland fishing.

A nobby *Cushag*, PL41, and a half-decker for Ramsey followed in 1908. By 1909 they were launching from the Peel Mill Yard where more nobbies were being built. *Vervine Blossom*, PL65, was launched in 1910, later with the addition of a 12hp Dan engine and by this time they had altered the traditional shape of the nobby by curving the sternpost and producing a canoe stern.

Peel's second steam drifter, again for Mr Egner and slightly smaller at 85ft than the *Manx Princess*, was the *Manx Bride*, launched in April 1911.

The same year came more 'motor-fitted fishing boats', such as the *Hidden Treasure* with her 24hp Bolinder engine for Arklow owners. Several nobbies were launched that year with increasing engine power. One, a 46ft nobby, had a Skandia engine. However, yet again, most boats seemed to be built for Irish owners. Sizes increased and in 1912 they launched a 60ft fishing boat with a 60hp Gardner engine for Irish owners.

A further launch was made in January 1913 when 'a fishing yacht built to the orders of James, William Henry and Charles Cowell gracefully took to the water. This was the *Gien Mie*, PL83, a half-decker built for cod long-lining and mackerel lining. In later life she had her counter stern chopped off and a transom added, perhaps to reduce her overall length for, when surveyed in 1993 she was 44ft overall yet was 47ft at launch.

One of the last nobbies was the 57ft *Lucy Mary*, launched in 1914 for Irish owners. During the war a limited staff was retained and in the 1920s they built various motor launches and yachts.

At some point they'd also taken over the old Watson's yard across the river and had to contract as business decreased. However they persevered on until one partner, William Watterson died in 1939 at the age of 70 and the firm finally closed for business, bringing to the end over a century of ship and boatbuilding in Peel.

Once the fish was landed the discussions amongst the fishermen began! The baskets are quarter-cran baskets which were the official measure of the amount of herring.

Fishermen and their Customs

Fishermen have, from days long gone, been a superstitious lot. You might say that to let such matters dictate the way of your life is just stupid, but spend your working days at the mercy of the elements at sea, and you might just start to see why most held such 'crazy' beliefs. Just remember that fishing is, and always has been, the most dangerous of occupations, a hazard even in calm waters where snaking ropes can take the unwitting person over the side and straight to the bottom. And statistics don't help: it is estimated that more than 6,000 trawlermen from Hull alone perished between 1835 and 1980. In one month alone in 1968, 58 men drowned in what has been dubbed 'the Triple Trawler Tragedy' off Iceland.

Scrubbing the hull of a nickey. Fishermen were always very proud of their boats and each boat would be annually beached for cleaning the hull and attending to any problems.

So spare a minute and understand why a man might turn home if, when leaving his house, he encounters a Minster of the faith, or 'black coat', as he would be referred to. Or why some animals are never referred to by their real names when at sea. Or why you should never 'whistle up the wind'.

The Manx fishers were no different to those from the rest of the UK, even those much further afield on mainland Europe and beyond. A fisherman would never turn back on a Monday even if he'd forgotten something at home, as then all the week would go wrong, although one wonders what happened if he encountered a Minister that day! Even encountering a woman could make him go home. This was in the days before women worked at the fishing. Red-haired women were especially unlucky, as were Roman Catholic priests. Referring to individual animal names whilst aboard was taboo. Cats were *scayheyder* in Manx (scratcher) and hares *yn fer lesh eleaych liauyr* (fellow with long lugs). If you by mistake mentioned one of these, then 'cold iron' must be touched in the way that today we say 'touch wood'. Never talk about rats though mention of fairies was fine.

Fairies were a sign of good luck as Manx folk know today. According to one 'old worthy' in a newspaper report of 1903 when recounting fishing of one hundred years before: "In old times we used to build our boats in the country near trees – timber where the fairies were taken was right lucky to build with them." He had added that when the boat was ready to be caulked, it was turned over with the sun. Indeed, whenever steering a boat out of the harbour, they would always steer with the sun. As one person put it, "the boat must always go with the sun". The same 'old worthy' mentioned how, if one boat was doing well at the fishing, then another would try and steal a herring basket, or ideally the tally stick, to bring them luck.

Another sign of luck was seeing the herring caterpillar, the *Braddagh Mollagh* in Manx, which appeared in August. If it was spotted going towards a house, or around one, then it was a sure sign of good herring fishing that night. Neither salt nor fire must be given out from the boat or bad luck will come.

No one was allowed to look over the side when hauling in the nets, except the last man who was pulling up. This old fellow recounted how he'd get a 'polt' in the head for 'keeking' over the side.

If you look back far enough, some of the superstitions were based on pagan rituals. Cleansing the planking of the boat with fire to drive out the evil spirits was commonplace.

William Cashen, assistant Peel harbourmaster in the late nineteenth century wrote of the customs of Manx fishermen of the 1850s.[17] He recounted how the fishermen began to prepare their boats by launching them off the bank of the river at Peel at the spring equinox, all helping each other. A jar of rum was shared and when launched, they shouted *"Lesh-ee! lesh-ee! lesh-ee!"* (With her! with her! with her!).

The huge piles of cotton nets were what the boats carried and set each night, and these had to be constantly maintained because of rips and rot.

Once in the water they could fit their sails and take the nets aboard, ready to go.

At the start of the season each fisherman chose a particular pub where he would receive credit throughout the season, both for him and his family and all his crew and their families. The bill would be settled up at the end of the season unless payments were made in-between.

When sailing out of the harbour, at a signal from the skipper, they'd remove their hats and offer up a silent prayer. Once out at sea and the Calf of Man and other headlands were in view, they'd open up a bottle of rum and each crew member would have a slug from the horn measure. Then they'd search for the natural appearances of the herring. Indeed, many fishermen watched in earnest whilst ashore and they often knew where the herring were before they left harbour by watching the gannets and seagulls. Then they'd wait for the Admiral's flag to be lowered, or the sun. One way to judge the darkness was when they couldn't see the black in their thumbnails when arms outstretched. Then they'd shoot the nets. One way of seeing if herring were nearby was by knocking the deck with a heavy object. If there were fish, the water would turn milky white.

When the Peel men were fishing the 'Big Bay' between Niarbyl and the Calf, sunrise was judged to have arrived when the sun broke over *Cronk-ny-Arrey-Lhaa* (the hill of the Rising Sun). The crew would be roused and hauling begun, before raising sail and heading home, finding a buyer on route or once back in Peel. Finally, they'd celebrate with more rum! However, as the years went by, the Temperance Party had gained influence and the tendency to drink at sea disappeared. However, the fights on the quay that supposedly happened frequently in the 1850s didn't. Even today, although seldom, a fisherman is known to have drink in his belly and to become rebellious and heavy fisted!

Manx Through and Through

The postwar period saw a series of new motorised 47ft fishing boats built for the Island, these all having the prefix of 'Manx'.

The first of these was the *Manx Fairy*, PL43, in 1937, having been built by the East Fife Boatbuilding Company at Cellardyke, on Scotland's east coast. This was quickly followed by the second, *Manx Beauty*, PL35, from the same yard the following year. At the same time two more were being built by J.&G. Forbes of Sandhaven, Fraserburgh. *Manx Lad*, PL23, and *Manx Lass*, PL33, arrived on the Island late in 1937. Once *Manx Beauty* had arrived, all four were blessed at a naming ceremony at Peel, all the boats being owned by the Isle of Man Fisheries Company of Peel, and built with

Manx Belle.

Manx Clover and
Manx Rose alongside
at Peel.

Manx Rose and *Manx
Clover* unloading
opposite the castle in
Peel.

finance through mortgages from the Manx Fisheries Board, a department of government.

Around the same time four more similar boats were commissioned by the same company from the yard of J. Tyrrell and Sons, Arklow, though the onset of war delayed their building process. *Manx Lily*, PL34, arrived first in 1940, followed by *Manx Clover*, PL47, and *Manx Fuchsia*, PL46, in 1941, *Manx Rose*, PL48, the following year and, finally, *Manx Belle*, PL62, in 1943.

The first boats were requisitioned for active war operations and *Manx Lad* sank off Holyhead in August 1940 whilst in service. *Manx Lily* had the tragic loss of two skippers within three years, both from Peel, and the boat was wrecked off Dippen Point, near Carradale in February 1948. However the rest of these boats seemed to have had long careers at the fishing. *Manx Beauty* and *Manx Fuchsia* were both sold off the Island in 1952 though the former is still afloat in Birkenhead. *Manx Fairy* then left for Liverpool in 1973 and was subsequently converted for pleasure and is now in Kess, Denmark. *Manx Lass* went to Runcorn and *Manx Belle* to Fleetwood, after which she went into private hands in 1991 and was broken up on the island of Paxos, Greece in 1998.

Manx Beauty in Birkenhead where she still survives.

Manx Clover in Ramsey with some of the crew and DJs from Radio Caroline. That's Dave Lee Travis on the right.

Finally *Manx Clover* and *Manx Rose* both moved to Caernarfon in 1983 and became pleasure boats in 1990 and 1991 respectively. *Manx Rose* is today a hulk lying on Dulas beach, to the northeast of Anglesey, whilst *Manx Clover* made various trips back to the Isle of Man in the 1990s but was eventually broken up at Peel in 2002.

In 1958 the *Manx Maid* arrived from Thomson's yard in Buckie to join the fleet of the Watterson family of Port Erin, and was a different type of vessel, having a forward wheelhouse. Amongst those also owned by the Wattersons was *Heather Maid*, CT19, built by Nobles of Fraserburgh in 1965 and which is still working from the Island.

Look around the various ports – Peel, Ramsey, Douglas, Castletown and Port St. Mary – and readers will see all manner of colourful fishing boats today. Some of these are

Manx Clover sailing off Peel during the
1994 Peel Traditional Boat Weekend.

Herring boats moored at Port St. Mary in the 1950s.

Scottish ringers in Peel in the mid-1960s. Front row: *Sapphire*, BA174, *Saffron*, BA182 & *Boys Pride*, B432 with *Bonnie Lass*, B69, lying behind. The ringers were renowned for their beautiful shape and varnished hulls.

old girls, as they say, and most are today scalloping. My favourite is *Frey*, CT137, based at Peel. She was built by the famous west coast yard of Nobles of Girvan where many lovely canoe-sterned ringers began their lives. Launched in 1972 as *Boy Ken*, TT70, she was first registered in Tarbert and then Oban before moving to the Island in 1979. She's simply a lovely example of that type of varnished ring-net boat, once so commonplace around the Island, and indeed the whole of the Irish Sea and west coast of Scotland.

Frey, CT137, was built in 1972 and is still fishing, here with scallop dredges. She's often to be seen in either Peel or Ramsey. (photo courtesy of Darren Purves)

The Kipperhouses of Peel

Walking along the quay at Peel on a January morning, it was impossible not to spot the smoke wafting over the roof top of the large group of buildings by the road bridge over the river. Almost immediately the unmistakable pungent smell of smoke hits the nostrils and the trail leads me along the road to the buildings. This is, of course, Moores, the one remaining smokehouse producing what I call proper kippers in the traditional Manx way. They've been smoking since 1882 and today little has changed though the fish are split by machine and they are smoked using pine sawdust. If anything, it is the quantity of demand that has changed the most.

Paul Desmond and his wife today run Moores Kipperhouse and it would seem more of a labour of love than any serious attempt at richness. Talking to Paul, it would seem he was simply eager to keep the tradition alive. He

Old wooden kipper box.

Keig's Kippers in about 1905.

Herring lassies washing their aprons, and probably themselves, on the beach at Port St. Mary.

remembers, after passing his driving test at 16, driving down from Ramsey, where his family had a fish shop, to pick up boxes of kippers. The family had moved onto the Island in the 1940s after coming over for a holiday. The premises seem to have had various owners and shut down in the 1980s until the Desmonds bought them in the late 1990s.

Before about 1770 all Manx herrings were either eaten fresh or salted down. With bounties being paid on barrelled herring and red herrings in mainland Britain, the idea of smoking fish was then introduced to the Island. It was a Mr. John Woodhouse who was the first person to erect a Red Herring House and introduce the Yarmouth method of curing red herrings by immersing them in smoke for many hours. It took another 170 years or so before the kipper was 'invented' by

Moore's Kipper House in Peel is the only smokehouse producing Manx kippers in the time-honoured way.

John Woodger at Seahouses, Northumberland, in 1843. When experimenting with salmon, he, it seems, was the first to split a herring by cutting it down the back and butterflying it so that the belly acts as a hinge, before briefly salting the fish and then smoking it for many hours. No one is quite sure when the first kipper was smoked on the Island but it is assumed it was practised in a small way until Kelsalls was established at Peel in 1880. Holdsworth wrote that little curing was done on the Island in 1877 with fresh fish being transported by vessel to the market at Liverpool. By 1900 Manx Kippers were a highly sort after commodity.

The kilns are run by burning sawdust on the floor just in the same way as they have for 130 years. Other smokehouses use electrical kilns.

When we left the herring fishery in an earlier chapter, when fishermen primarily set after scallops and queenies, it would appear that herring fishing completely disappeared

The old fish-splitting machine splits and guts 60 herring in a minute which is much quicker than by hand!

from Manx waters. That's not quite right though, with the opening of the scallop fishery in the 1960s, the last of the boats working drift-nets finished. Scottish ringers continued into the 1970s when they were replaced with mid-water trawlers. With the closure of the North Sea herring by the European Commission, there was more pressure on the Irish Sea though, mostly, by vessels owned outside the Island. A brief flurry of activity occurred between 1977 and 1979. Today all the herring quota is fished by Northern Ireland boats landing into Kilkeel and the Manx herring fishery is as good as over. All we are left with is memories of a hotpot of herring and potatoes.

Moores has seven kilns which are capable of smoking 20,000 herrings in each. The herring was split by hand, a long tedious job. In the 1880s there were over 100 people working on site and it wasn't until the 1950s that the first herring splitting machine was installed. In the 1970s there were still five kilns on the go and the tedious work was undertaken by herring girls from Southern Ireland. 100 cran of fish was being smoked then each weekday and occasionally on Saturday.

Today Paul uses only one kiln as the demand for kippers has fallen. He smokes twice a week during the summer and once in winter. Now it's 2000 to 3000 herring at a time, smoking high up in the kiln. The cast iron, solid-looking splitting machine, made by Fisadco Ltd, still works perfectly and can split a fish every second. The herring are then cleaned and brined for ten minutes before being hung on tenterhooks and placed high up in the kiln, probably some 15 feet above the floor of the smoker where six piles of pine sawdust are lit. They smoke for some six to eight hours before becoming traditional Manx Kippers smoked the way they always have been. There are other producers of kippers on the Island, but they all use electric kilns these days and, to me, a kipper smoker myself, the taste is just not the same. Paul sells his finished product in his shop, along with smoked bacon, and his traditional Manx Kippers are available from him by post on his website. The sad part is the fact that all the herrings are imported, mostly from Scotland in Paul's case. Which means that Manx folk still have their very own kippers and strawberry jam sandwiches still fixed firmly on their menu!

Kipper sign on the main shopping drag in Douglas.

Smoke emerging from the top of the kiln. There are seven kilns in all though such a number are never needed these days.

The Fishermen's Mission

Fishermen through the ages have been considered as a group of working people almost outside of society. In the eighteenth and nineteenth centuries, in some towns they were literally pushed to the fringes of that town to live in unsatisfactory hovels, they being regarded as smelly and fighting folk. Before mechanisation, given the nature of the job, it's not surprising that the stench of fish followed them, and many fishing communities had an overspill of drinking establishments, so the latter was common enough. But when tragedy struck – and with fishing being the most dangerous of occupations, and still is, this was quite often – there was little or no help from the authorities who simply would have preferred them to go away.

In Britain the Royal National Mission to Deep Sea Fishermen was formed in 1881 and before that various groups tried to turn fishermen's unsavoury habits, such as the heavy drinking, about. Boats even sailed out into the North Sea offering spiritual help whilst the boats fished. In fact early mission boats sailed under banners such as 'Preach the Word' and 'Heal the Sick'. Conditions on the whole were pretty bad for fishermen in those days,

In the Isle of Man it was generally left to the fishermen, who were pretty much farmer/fishermen until 1840, to offer help amongst themselves in times of need. But the advent of lifeboats offered some reassurance. Although a lifeboat was established in Douglas in 1803, it was lost a decade later. The Royal National Institution of the Preservation of Life at Sea (forerunner of the RNLI) was founded in 1824 by Sir William Hillary who actually lived on the Island in a house overlooking Douglas Bay. Within two years there were two boats at Douglas and by the end of the decade there were boats added at Castletown, Peel and Ramsey. Not only were lifeboatmen able to come to the aid of sinking vessels, they

Opposite: The Tower of Refuge on St. Mary's Rock in Douglas Bay which was funded by Sir William Hillary and, until recently, permanently stocked with blankets and water for any seafarer in distress. Hillary founded The Royal National Institution of the Preservation of Life at Sea (forerunner of the RNLI).

Two boats from the
Firth of Forth in Peel
inner harbour. Boats
from many parts of
the UK coast joined in
with the Manx herring
fishing. The boats are
Gratitude, LH28, and
Providence, LH80.

also offered more practical help at times of tragedy and did so
during the course of the next hundred and seventy years.
Throughout this time the government generally stood still
and did nothing when life was lost.

It wasn't until 1996 that a Fishermen's Mission was
established by Erik White in the Island, this being a branch of
the main UK Mission and part of the Northern Ireland region.
However, unlike the UK missions who employed full-time
officers, this was a totally voluntary organisation and if
anything, money passed from the Island to the UK mission in

the form of donations, not the other way round.

On the 15th October 1998, Michael Craine, born and bred a Manxman, was driving along the south of the Island when he witnessed the sinking of the fishing boat *Amber Rose*, B417, several miles off Port St. Mary in calm weather.

"It was in an area of notorious rip tides," he said. "I saw the vessel roll onto her side and capsize and go down by her stern."

He immediately alerted the Coastguard who then deployed the lifeboat and Mike watched as the lifeboat headed south instead of southwest. Mike phoned the Coastguard again and through a series of messages managed to point the lifeboat in the right direction which eventually picked up four casualties from the water although, tragically, the skipper drowned. Mike ended up in the hospital to get information about the casualties and there met Erik White, and he immediately decided there and then to join the mission.

Mike lived on the promenade in Peel and was brought up amongst the days of the varnished ringers in the harbour and their landings of herring. He was even a page boy one year for the Peel Herring Queen. He recalls being on the Peel breakwater one day in 1968 and seeing two fishing boats – the steel *Captain Hardy*, LO96, and the wooden *Faithlie*, A100, and being intrigued in how different they were although they were both just 'fishing boats'. From that time he got the bug and started listing every boat he saw on the Island and even today records them, wherever he goes on holiday around the globe. He was in the Merchant Navy after school and worked as a radio operator on vessels such as the *Othello* off Iceland in 1974, between the Cod Wars. Before he joined the navy he got a job at the kipperhouse of Alex Reid, a Buckie fisherman who'd moved to the Island and owned his two boats and started kippering. He said that it was Alex who was a mine of information. When he returned after his time in the navy he became a TV engineer. But, having a healthy respect for fishermen and experiencing a spell off Iceland, I guess, it was no surprise that he joined the Fishermen's Mission.

In December 2014 the Isle of Man separated from the UK Mission by mutual agreement and thus became The Fishermen's Mission Isle of Man. This suited them better as they work in very different ways. Now all funds raised stay on the Island and are used to help local fishermen and their families just as much as they provide in times of need for visiting fishermen from anywhere around the world. It is the only charity which focuses on fishermen and their needs. However, they are still affiliated to the UK body so that they can seek advice and additional support where needed.

The Isle of Man Mission is run on a completely voluntary basis so that all the money raised is used to provide welfare. It is available at all times of need and because of the small size of its committee, decisions can be made quickly. Incidents, which can happen at any time, are usually attended to within thirty minutes of them being reported. Then they can target the immediate requirements, whether financial, practical or pastoral.

Today Mike is the Mission's Agent and Welfare Officer, and is joined on the committee by the chairman, the treasurer, secretary, minister and two others. Over the last four years they have contacted nine bereaved families, met with 350 fishermen, given financial support to 23 emergencies, attended to the aftermath of two sinkings, attended 15 promotional events, made 120 welfare visits, supported 29 life-changing injuries and two children and distributed £13,000. In 2017 alone this was £3,700. They have also distributed some 240 PFD (Personal Floatation Devices) with financial help from the Manx Government, and these they then service.

So what exactly does that mean, I asked.

"For example," Mike answered. "We offer assistance and support when a fishermen dies. Things like living expenses for the bereaved family. Help out arranging funerals or more mundane things like the gas bill, or give them food vouchers. Help anyone not get evicted. Get emergency accommodation by finding a hotel for a visiting fisherman. Get a taxi to take him there. Or we can help filling in forms. Everyone knows how difficult it is to sort out benefits from the DHSS. Or we can lessen loneliness with home or hospital visits, even going as far as, this year, making a prison visit. Visit retired fishermen, and cheer them up with a box of chocolates or whatever. We regard ourselves as a friendly face at times of distress. We have contacts with the Dreadnought specialised hospital charity and have helped two local fishermen get treatment there for back troubles. Then there's the daily things people need. I remember one fisherman who phoned to say he was having difficulty saving money to buy a new settee but was embarrassed when friends called round. When I visited I found all the springs and webbing in his chair and settee broken and so we arranged for funds to replace them. In another instance there was a terminally ill fisherman who needed his bed sheets and clothes washing daily and given that their washing machine had seen better days, we

Two local Peel boats – *Constant Friend*, PL61 and *Venture Again*, PL39, in Ramsey harbour for the queenie scallop season in August 2017.

purchased a replacement for the family."

I asked for an example of a day-to-day action.

"For example, when the *Evara*, N27, sank in Port Erin, I tried to talk to the skipper. But he was traumatised and uncommunicative. From the crewmen I managed to find out what happened and what they needed. Returning half an hour later with coffee and cakes, I broke the ice and managed to arrange accommodation and meals for the two men. Next day the leak was repaired and the vessel towed back to Kilkeel. When the *Molly*, KY1030 was towed into Peel the crew were covered in black oil after trying to repair the engine. I bought towels and toiletries for them and arranged showers in the marina. Then we gave them funds to buy meals and stores for the boat. Or the *Eschol*, M220, on passage from Scotland to North Wales. She came into Peel after a gale warning was issued. But the skipper had lost his wallet in Scotland and with it being a bank holiday, couldn't get funds from his bank. So the Mission gave them funds to cover their stay in Peel. All little stuff but to the fishermen they made a difference."

One of the saddest incidents Mike recounted was about the Ghanian fisherman Mark. Mark was working a 15-month contract aboard a Scottish scalloper which called into Peel. He was employed on an eight-hours-on-two-hours-off basis for £850 a month and wasn't allowed to leave the vessel because in actuality he was an 'illegal' with no paperwork. This modern-day slavery has been the recent subject of concern, with questions being asked in the House of Commons. It seems that many come from outside Europe with promises of work on cruise liners, only to end up fishing. They have no experience and find themselves in a foreign culture with foreign food. Mike met Mark who wanted to leave, but after recounting his treatment Mike contacted the Mission Officer in Troon who had experience of this. But Mike could only offer two choices: Get no income and be arrested staying on land or go back to his boat and work out his contract.

Funding comes from various quarters, though not from government. The Manx Fish Producers Organisation donates annually as do the fishermen each Christmas. There's an annual Quiz which helps to keep a good rapport between the Mission and the fishermen as well as raising money. There are a number of groups that help out such as The Shipwrecked Mariner's Society or the Round Table. Locally 'Housing Matters' donate from their food bank whilst 'Cafe Lingo' help out with language translating.

For fishermen the Mission is a place of sanctuary, a place where they can trust they will not be turned away at times of distress. They also promote sea safety, being part of the Manx Fishing Industry Safety Group. Their great work was recognised in 2014 when they won the 'Isle of Man Newspaper Excellence Award for Charity, Cultural and Social Enterprise'. Theirs is a cause worthy of recognition, and the work Mike does is vitally important. And what does he get out of it?

"Just happy to see a smile on a face of a traumatised fishermen a few days down the line after the trauma."

The work carries on regardless and one is brought down to reality when passing the chandlery in Peel. There's a notice on the door regarding the latest casualty for the fishing industry: the *Nancy Glen*, TT100, was lost not far from her home port of Tarbert on the 18th January 2018, a week before we'd spoken. Although one crew member survived, two others went down with the boat. Relatives were wanting to raise the boat to recover the bodies but, at that stage, the authorities were refusing to pay so it was left to organisations to ask for donations to cover the cost that was at first said would exceed £60,000 (it will probably be ten times that in the end). [However, just as this book was going to print, the Scottish government had stepped in so that, along with crowdfunding by the Clyde Fishermen's Association, the money was provided which then enabled the vessel to be brought to the surface by a lifting barge and the two fishermen's bodies recovered.] The Fishermen's Mission Isle of Man was asking for such donations so they could contribute to the fund. The same notice reminded me that such tragedy is not without recent history in the Island when the *Solway Harvester* sank in 2000 with the loss of seven lives. It goes without saying that the work of the Mission is therefore vital for fishermen everywhere.

POSTSCRIPT

During our talk Mike mentioned a book called 'Fish and Ships', one that I confused with another of the same title that I have on my shelves. Ironically, an hour after I left him I found myself in a secondhand book shop in Peel, staring at the book he'd referred to, not the one I thought he was talking about. This one was an autobiography by Belgian-born Angela Kneale who came to the Island after the Second World War, married to a Manxman. From 1957 onwards to the 1980s, she helped many a French or Dutch fisherman who found himself in distress on the Island. Although she held no official position as far as the Manx were concerned, she was appointed French Consular Agent in the Isle of Man in 1964. Reading the back of the book, I was amazed to see that there were between 300 and 400 French and Dutch trawlers working the Irish Sea in the post war period. It's a fascinating story.

Fish-Inspired Art

If you consider colonies of art such as the Newlyn School from Cornwall, it's obvious that the working lives of fishermen and their boats conjure up both the true grit of the job at hand, and the romanticism associated with it, although most would wonder where this sentimental romance originated from. Nevertheless fishing boats, which today tend to be colourful whereas in the past they were the opposite, in drab colours (yet still managed to instil nostalgia), have attracted artists the world over. That has to be a Good Thing, given paintings can be a source of historical evidence. That they continue to do so adds to the general consensus that art moves society onwards.

Manx artists are no exception, and there are many outlets where their work can be viewed and purchased. But aside from the galleries and tourist shops, art in the open can be more invigorating.

One such Manx artist who has over the last couple of years inspired is Nicola Dixon from Peel. Having been painting maritime scenes spanning 30 years, and having sailed on a variety of sailing boats, she was commissioned by the Isle of Man Post Office to produce a range of stamps for their Green Mann – Food Matters, described as a 'delicious set of six stamps celebrating the Island's landscape and the horticultural, farming and fishing heritage and our diverse group of food producers'. Six highly colourful originals with one entitled 'Fish to Dish' showing a modern potter, a harbour and various shellfish. The whole set is evocative of the reality of food

Peel Traditional Boat Weekend 'T' shirt and poster design 2012 (PL12 on the boat) by Nicola Dixon.

culture on the Island.

Nicola then went on to produce an art installation decorating the main carpark in the centre of Peel. Twelve metal panels, entitled the 'Deer's Cry', also referred to as 'St Patrick's Breastplate' or 'The Lorica of St Patrick', have been erected to shield the car park from the road.

Postcard from the Isle of Man – 'Farm to Yarn' and 'Fish to Dish' – by Nicola Dixon.

In her own words these were a labour of love on which she spent a year working.

Nicola with her steel panels shielding Peel's main car park. (photo courtesy of Simon Park)

"The lines I chose to work with," she says, "are: 'I arise today, through strength of heaven, light of sun, radiance of moon, splendour of fire, speed of lightning, swiftness of wind, depth of the sea, stability of earth and firmness of rock.' They really place you in the environment, and in nature which I thought was great for Peel, because Peel is one of those places where there are always people. You look up and there's

always someone on the hill, or on the beach, or on the breakwater. The depth of sea is shown as the life under the sea, the stability of the earth is shown as the Manx landscape, the view up the coast and the firmness of rock is shown as St Patrick's Isle."

She also included the history of boats coming to Peel, with Viking boats, followed by Manx nickeys, herring drifters and the motorised fishing boats. For the sea life there's seals, Minke whales, herring, queenies and basking sharks. Twelve panels, then, that tell the history of Peel.

"There has been a lot of heart and soul put into this. It had to be right for Peel," she added. And, judging by the comments I heard just in the short time I was there, it is just right for Peel too.

Panel detail of steam trawler.

Night-time view of
our panel landscape
illuminating Peel's
breakwater from the
castle as part of the
Deer's Cry.

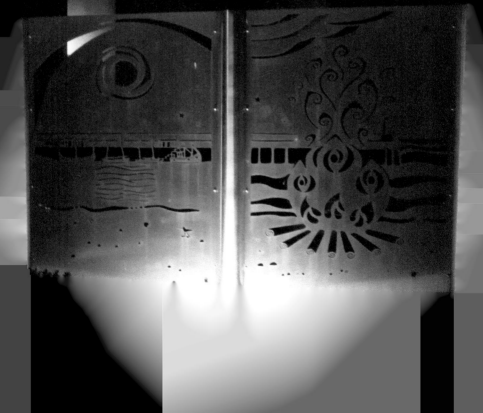

Lobsters, Crabs, Whelks and Other Things

Lobsters and crabs have been a part of the Manx fishery almost as far back as any documents go. Given the rich grounds off much of the coast, the earliest dwellers found these a source of great nutrition. Only with the transportation of fish across to the mainland, did shellfish become an established fishery.

It was, of course, the crofter/fishermen who first set withy pots in the shallows around the rocky coasts. Most of the beaches would have had some activity in this direction. The pots were homemade, and one report mentions 'baskets made of twigs'. Small rowboats were used to set them on individual ropes, attached to some kind of buoy. Buoys were often made from inflated pigs' bladders and in many cases the inflated skins of dogs. Willow was best, and these were collected: good straight ones could be had at Greeba. Bait used was mackerel or whatever was available, and salted fish when fresh wasn't.

I'm getting as red as a lobster at

PORT ST. MARY, I.O.M.

Lobster postcard from the Isle of Man.

111

Lobster pots at Douglas.

Pots were traditionally made from willow before the more modern pot.

The Claugues, according to Alan Kermode, were the last to fish from the beach at Niarbyl in the 1940s[18]. Today the beach there is quiet, except for the odd holidaymaker and some film makers when I was there in August 2017. Commercial potting is left to just a handful of boats working from the main ports. These tend to work trains of pots, up to 20 in a train, marked each end with a buoy. Agreement between the scallopers and the potters mean that both know where the other work. In winter, when the lobsters go out into deeper water, the pots move, and the scallopers avoid. It's a scenario that works well.

For the recreational lobster and crab potter – and there are more of these than commercial potters – a licence has to be bought (currently £30). These potters may fish up to 5 pots, the maximum catch per day is two lobsters (but no more that seven lobsters per week) and five crabs. They cannot fish outside the three mile limit and have to submit returns on what they catch. They must adhere to the same minimum landing sizes as commercial fishermen which state that the carapace of a lobster must be 87mm or more in length. A crab must be 130mm across the shell at the widest point. Furthermore it is illegal in the Isle of Man to take, land, sell or have in possession any crab or lobster that is 'berried', i.e. is carrying eggs that are developing. Any berried crabs or lobsters must be returned to the water immediately. The taking of v-notched lobsters is also illegal. All these measures are to ensure sustainability of supply and are the same through the UK, albeit occasionally with different minimum landing sizes.

For whelk fishing, controls on the amount to be fished have only recently come into effect throughout the 12-mile limit, mostly by limiting the number of whelk pots that can be fished as well as the issuing of specific licences. Previously it was only within the three-mile limit. The vast majority of whelks landed are exported to Asia where they are deemed a popular dish.

Oysters were once brought to purpose-built 'beds' at Port Soderick where they were sold to the tourists. Today the remains of the walls of the tanks – which is what they consisted of – can be seen in the southern corner of the bay, along with plenty of empty oyster shells

Maughold Head lighthouse with the fishing grounds beyond.

The steel potter *New Dawn*, PL1, coming into Peel. This modern type of boat was built by Grimsby-based shipbuilders Harris & Garrod Ltd in 2006 as *Genesis II*, SH300.

Castletown harbour looking inland from the top of the castle. Castletown is a drying harbour.

Whelks!

dotted about. The majority of the oysters seem to have been imported from Ireland, especially Strangford Lough. Today, although Strangford Lough oysters are few and far between, they are still regarded by some connoisseurs to be the very best oysters in the world.

Whelk pots at Ramsey looking over the harbour to where the fishing boats are moored.

The remains of the oyster tanks at Port Soderick.

FURTHER READING

For a full insight into the workings of the Isle of Man herring fishery, I suggest getting hold of a copy of the 1991 *Manx Sea Fishing* which is a collection of 12 information cards, 7 documents and a resource book, all of which was produced for schools by Manx National Foundation. It's a really excellent publication. This, and other sources to visit, have been listed in the endnotes.

For books, the following are worthy:

Callister, T. *The Herring Fishery of the Isle of Man* (1815)
Moore, A.W. *A History of the Isle of Man* (1900)
Smith, W.C. *A Short History of the Irish Seas Herring Fisheries during the Eighteenth and Nineteenth Centuries* (1923)

Mason, J. *Scallop and queen fisheries in the British Isles* (1929)
Palmer, F. *Glimpses of Old Peel* (1993)
Palmer, F. *Peel Three* (2009)
Teare, M. *Sail-room Stories*; a set of 3 pamphlets – 'Sailmaking', 'Ships Chandlers', 'Ice, salt and smoke' (2014)

For more generalised fishing history, about Manx fishing boats and that of the ring-net:

Holdsworth, E.W.H. *Deep-Sea Fishing and Fishing Boats* (1874)
March, E. *Sailing Drifters* (1952)
Martin, A. *The Ring-Net Fishermen* (1981)
Miller, N. *The Lancashire Nobby* (2009)
Smylie, M. *Traditional Fishing Boats of Britain & Ireland* (1999)
Smylie, M. *Herring – a History of the Silver Darlings* (2004)

ENDNOTES

1. Blundell, William. Manx Society, vol XXV (1876).

2. Harrison, W. *An Account of the Loss of the Manx Herring Fleet*, 1872. Manx Museum Archive M0773/8 (a league is three nautical miles).

3. The actual number has been quoted as 300 and 400, with the lower perhaps being more realistic though nothing is certain.

3. *Tour of a Lady's Voyage from England to Ireland*, pp46-62, 1802. MM Archive MS05875A

4. Letter dated 30/11/1776 from Lords of the Admiralty to Earl of Suffolk in *Atholl Papers*

5. Moore, A.W., *History of the I-O-M*, chap 2 – Fishing

6. 1864 *Royal Commissioners' Inquiries into the Sea Fisheries of the United Kingdom*

7. *Tour of a Lady's Voyage from England to Ireland'*, pp46-62, 1802. MM Archive MS05875A

8. 'A Night in a Herring Boat'. Manx Museum archive 04417/98

9. *Peel Two* by Fred Palmer.

10. 'Early Manx Fishing Craft' by Basil and Eleanor Megaw, in *The Mariner's Mirror*, vol 27, issue 2 1941.

11. Much of the information comes from 'Notes on the Lhane Moar and Largagh Districts of Kirk Andreas' by Thomas H. Kinrade, written in 1945 and published by Chiollagh Books of Onchan in 1993.

12. 'Manx Sea Fishing' resource book, p27, Manx Heritage Foundation, 1991.

13. Manx Museum archive FLS P.C.I./D

14. I read this on a board entitled 'Fishing the Niarbyl' in an exhibition at the church in Dalby in August 2017.

15. Palmer, F. *Glimpses of Old Peel*, 1993

16. Palmer, F. *Old Peel* (undated)

17. *Peel City Guardian*, 11th January 1896

18. Dalby Church 'Fishing the Niarbyl' exhibition, Aug 2017